Our Harry's War

1553 - Sgt. G.H. MORGAN

Royal Warwickshire Regiment
1914-1918

HENRY MORGAN

Published by
RYDAN Publishing 2002
17, Perryhill Drive, Little Sandhurst, Berkshire, GU47 8HS England

European Distribution
28, Route de Larmor, Pont Lorois, 56550 BELZ, France
e-mail <henry.morgan@freesbee.fr>

First published in 2002
Copyright © Henry Morgan 2002

ISBN 0-9542193-0-9

Printed by
The Chameleon Press Limited
5-25 Burr Road, London SW18 4SQ, England

Dedication

To my dear and loving sister Betty, who started this project
but never saw it completed.
(Recruiting Sergeant Elizabeth Mary Hunt - (Née Morgan)
ATS and WRAC
1926 - 1999

In the compilation, research and assembly of facts, from my
father's note books and remembered conversations,
I wish to acknowledge with grateful thanks
the following, for advice, help and invaluable information

The Imperial War Museum - London
Museum of the Royal Warwickshire Regiment - Warwick
Regimental Museum of the Queens Own Highlanders - Inverness
Commonwealth War Graves Commission - London
Public Records Office - London
"In Flanders Fields Museum" -Ypres
The Western Front Association

also
Pipe Major Peter Rankin and Birmingham Branch members of
The Seaforth Highlanders Regimental Association (1935 to 1943)
for my happy childhood recollections of Annual Dinners 'Piping the
Haggis' and gifts for we children, from Father Xmas, who I can confirm,
wears a Seaforth kilt under his red robe.

note
The added songs and poetry were learned from my parents, the words may
not be entirely correct. In the matter of the army versions, the words could
well have been 'watered down' for the benefit of their children's moral
education.

**Cover design and finished artwork
by Jane Shilling, née Morgan**
(*Grand-daughter*)

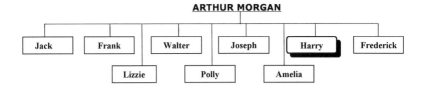

ARTHUR MORGAN

| Jack | Frank | Walter | Joseph | Harry | Frederick |

| Lizzie | Polly | Amelia |

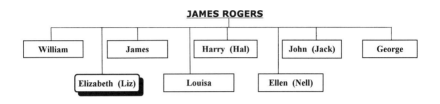

JAMES ROGERS

| William | James | Harry (Hal) | John (Jack) | George |

| Elizabeth (Liz) | Louisa | Ellen (Nell) |

Morgan & Rodgers Family tree

Harry and Liz

Introduction

Why has this true story taken such a long time in its telling? You may well ask. Is it not a fact that the very young know only one thing for certain and that is, mums are made to look after us and dads are made to mend things. Nothing else is of importance to the very young, and I was no exception.

I had heard talk of the war by my father Harry, at an early age, by my many uncles too, but thought that it must have been hundreds of years ago and of no interest to me. In fact it had ended only eleven years before my birth. I was also aware of numerous notebooks in a drawer, but they never appealed, or invited my curiosity.

My sister Betty first took my father's books, at his request, as late as 1950, and produced a typed-out synopsis, which was fortunate, for the originals were only prepared in pencil and were fading. He was overjoyed at having a professionally typed, brief, outline record of his wartime experiences, in addition to the notebooks and treasured it greatly. He simply wanted the information to go to us his two children, and had no further thoughts than that.

Harry died in 1964, and the documents were then held by my mother Liz, who died 16 years later in Coventry. They then passed back to Betty who, after a number of years thought I should have them.

Regrettably, and perhaps to my absolute shame, although I had the notebooks then, it was not until my retirement in 1994, that I looked at, and read them. I had been too engrossed in my own life to take an interest. Raising my family and work pressures, had fully occupied my time.

Why do we never take an interest in our past family history until all the people able to give vital information, are no longer with us? Perhaps, it is because so often, we more fortunate ones are sheltered by them, from the daily hardships and problems they suffer, purely and simply by virtue of their kindness and consideration to us, as children. We therefore cannot fully appreciate their trials and tribulations, until our own experiences of life, give awareness. By this time it is often too late to be acknowledged.

Although Harry's notes included the names of all officers and men, he expressly asked my sister not to name them in her typed outline. He did not wish to embarrass any members of their family, or destroy any favourable image they might have had of their loved ones. I have therefore, also respected his wishes and only those actions which were commendable carry their true names, all other names have been changed.

Here then, after visits to the battlefields of Flanders, and four years of research and writing, is Harry's true story:

Sorry I'm late, but this belongs to you, Dad!

Henry Morgan (Arthur)

One

Birmingham 1895 - *My Arrival*

To understand my motivation, and perhaps the reason for many of my later decisions, some reflection on the period, as well as my family circumstances may be of help. Conditions during my early years were far different to the present day, yet no less exciting.

Just two years before the Klondyke gold rush of 1897, and seven years after the construction of the first motor cars, the most important day of 1895 for me was 21 November when I was born. Christened George Henry Morgan, to the many people sharing my life, in true Brummie style, I would always be: 'Our Harry.'

We lived in the Ladywood district, which at that time was a rather 'rough cut' area of the City of Birmingham. Our family was a large one, which in itself was not significant. Large families were quite usual. In the absence of social assistance, and with a strong expectation of the breadwinner being unable to win bread, it was practical to have the additional support of extra wage earners.

My elder brother Jack was sixteen that same year, but in addition to Jack, there was Frank, Walter, and Joe. I also had three sisters Lizzie, Polly and Amelia, yet, as if the house was not already bursting at the seams, two years from now my youngest brother Fred would arrive, expanding the total to six boys and three girls.

Like everyone else in our social circle, we did not have much money. It therefore did not occur to us that we were poor. Everyone appeared to be on the same level, and being unused to luxuries, we never expected any. The world didn't owe us a living and we asked simply a repayment for any work we did. Work was easy to find in the city at that time, but choice was restricted.

Careers were for the wealthy, daily jobs were all we could expect. There would be the odd opportunity to do some painting, factory labouring, shop assisting, etc. If you worked well and the foreman or the boss found you to be favourable, sometimes the offer of a full time job would spring from a casual situation. Birmingham being a centre for industry meant that there was no shortage of factories, and a seemingly endless variety of products and processes.

Dad had been a farm worker in Stourport, having been a farmer's boy since the age of about 10 or 11yrs. He was canny enough to find odd jobs here and there and struggled to raise the family, brought to the big city in order to increase the work opportunities for the boys. Many were the difficulties in selecting a reasonable job, that paid sensible wages. Some that gave a good return were simply better kept away from.

On 4 May 1896, a new newspaper called 'The Daily Mail' was born and it started off, priced at a halfpenny, with powerful editorials to grab the attention of a new public. One of these on 29 July, dealt with the many hazards of a normal working day, the risks were obviously well enough known to the employers. It was most unusual for this sort of information, to be made known to the working man.

They spoke for instance of a limited period of ten years being the expected life for an operator working in an ice manufacturing environment, before pneumonia or consumption took him away. Of paint manufacturing, where workers handled lead and arsenic, bringing on lung or throat disease. House painters, and industrial paint contractors, mixing their materials and breathing in fumes to bring on painter's colic, lead paralysis, or worse.

Gilding, bronzing, or silvering of mirrors by use of mercury, rewarded workers with at first, a sign of trembling hands followed by sore mouth and gums, indicating a sure sign of mercuric poisoning. To leave his job or die, would be the only choice, usually however, he would carry on out of dire necessity. He would die if he stayed, yet could not survive or maintain a family without money if he left. It was a much restricted option and invariably they all stayed.

Bleaching and dyeing industries relied heavily upon Chlorine gas, the manufacture of which gave the workers producing it, merely some nine years life expectation. Even hat makers developed lung disease from the fine lint released from the materials they worked with. It was calculated that fewer men died as a result of making dynamite, than did curing hides for the leather industry. Matchmakers risked a particularly horrid disease that attacked their bones making them crumble, starting with the jaw and face.

Grinding metals caused asthma and affected air passages to nose and lungs. Worse than this was grinding needles, said to bring the worker death before reaching middle age. In all these instances and many more, there was little escape for those involved. How fortunate that my father had been a lowly farm worker, on poor pay of course, but working in the sweet fresh air all day long!

With nine children there is little need to describe my mother's job, except to say she did it well. Expectedly, this did not have much interest for me at that time, or in the first few years of my life, I was no doubt aware, only of pleasure and food, like all babies. Those around me however, were involved in everyday life and, as I grew older they talked about the many things happening. Eventually, I began to take in some of the information.

The horse road was still for horses. I had never seen a motor car and knew nothing of the Self-Propelled Traffic Association's efforts, to have the fourteen miles an hour speed restriction, imposed by Westminster, raised. They were quite certain that the new 'auto motor cars' would eventually replace horses.

In my second year of life 1897, the district and the whole country indeed, joined in the major celebrations, for the Diamond Jubilee of Her Majesty Queen Victoria. The jewellers of Birmingham struck 15 million medals and 6 million broaches. Attended by Royalty, dignitaries and soldiers from all over Europe, it was proposed to make the day, a permanent Bank Holiday in perpetuity. This was objected to, by the 'Coach and Axletree makers Association' of South Staffs, who claimed it was a bad idea because Bank Holidays caused injury to the working classes, a loss to their employers, and were a great inconvenience.

Public money was spent without caution, particularly in the capital. Spectator stands were built of such magnitude that some buildings were completely hidden from view, using about seventy-nine thousand tons of timber and six hundred tons of iron. They suggested that the seats, if connected together, would stretch from London to Eastbourne, about sixty four miles distant.

When England celebrated, it celebrated big. We had street parties with food for all, on trestle tables. Children's party games, competitions, prizes, and celebration mugs, tins of chocolates, flags and dancing. I am told I was there and that I enjoyed it all but, at under four years old I remember not a thing! Later on at school, the event was to be logged into National History lessons as being of 'historical importance.' I suppose this must have been the greatest celebration within the whole of my life that I attended, yet I remained unaware of it until school!

Of seemingly little significance, there was a report in April 1897 that the Boers in Africa were arming themselves with British revolvers. Messrs. Webley & Sons, of Weaman Street, Birmingham had a contract to supply 5000 of them. This was destined to mean much more, just two years later.

Other events grabbed the attention of people that year who marvelled at the boldness of engineers, completing a tunnel under the Thames. Named the Blackwall tunnel, it was opened, during May 1897 by The Prince of Wales, as her Majesty was away in the north of England. Taking five years to make, it was 6,200ft long and 17ft-6 inches high at the centre, with a road and two pavements. An exciting project, no one died, but many workers were injured, due to the new technique of using compressed air, to hold back the water. This enabled the men to clear away the solid chunk of earth, cut out by the boring machine.

In one particular part of the working, air-to-space proportion had been increased, to three and a half times the above ground level. It adversely affected 200 men over the total period. To speak, they had to shout, in order to make the air move and their voices heard, the sound they made, had a harder, higher and more nasal tone than was normal. Whistling was not possible. Neither, if they could afford one, was opening a champagne bottle with an audible pop, or lighting a cigarette without it burning away like a match.

They said that the workers knew it was the signal to get out into normal air, when they felt giddiness, or deafness, or if they bled from nose or ear. The change of environment whenever they did this, gave rise to a great lowering of temperature, and hot baths were always kept in readiness on the surface. Another risk they faced, was the 'bends' as experienced by deep sea divers, surfacing too quickly.

This achievable feat, made up somewhat, for the negative feelings previously given off, by what to many, was the too ambitious plan, to dig a tunnel under the English Channel, to France. A shareholder's meeting was called by The Channel Tunnel Co. in January 1897, at the Charing Cross Hotel, London, to advise that all work had been stopped. It was proposed to start again when the French were more friendly towards us!

Unrest meanwhile, prevailed in Africa over the next two years. A demand was received from the Transvaal government, for the immediate withdrawal of present British troops from their border. They also required the stoppage of further supplies and additional troops, with a stipulation that differences should be settled through an arbitrator.

It appears that we found this demand "Insolent" and an infringement of our rights to interfere on behalf of the Uitlanders. A short reply to this effect was dispatched by Sir Alfred Milner, and on 11 October 1899 the Boer War began.

During my infant years, and at school, I was to hear all about the glories of this period. Colonel Baden-Powell and the town of Mafeking, and Lieutenant Winston Churchill, war correspondent for the Morning Post.

Patriotism was strong and formed a large part of our daily diet. My brothers at school had the morning papers read to them each day, and they returned home to pass the news on to my father and mother.

It was yet another big day, for the funeral of Her Majesty Queen Victoria, who died at 6.30pm on 22 January 1901. Her close Court went into 1 year of full mourning. The whole of the country seemed to go into mourning, with almost everyone wearing black. Schools and many businesses closed for the day. I was then five and seem vaguely to remember it. Our new Monarch was to be His Majesty King Edward VII.

By 5 April 1902, there was news of a new Motor War-Car made for Vickers, Sons and Maxim. Designed for coastal defense over rough ground, fully iron clad with a $16^1/_2$ HP motor and a speed of 9 mph. Able to support a load of 12 tons, carry fuel for 200 miles and be driven and steered by just one man. This was even more incredulous than the recently announced news of the motor cycle that could reach a speed of 40 mph.

I found all these mechanical things fascinating though I had no leanings towards doing anything mechanical. They were exciting to many schoolchildren. When later at the age of 8 yrs, I was told that two Americans named Wilber and Orville Wright, at a strange sounding place called Kittyhawk, had actually flown through the sky in a balloonless airship, I found it breathtaking.

This took place on Friday 18 December 1903. Our teacher read it out to us from a daily paper. The airship had propellers and was driven by a motor engine. No one really appreciated the full implication of this, or the effect it would finally have on the world.

Osler Street Birmingham, was my school. A standard school of the day giving a basic education, we had all been there. We had what we got, and were satisfied because we could aim no higher. The days were uneventful and success at most things eluded me. Our learning was by what they called the 'rote' system, whereby we repeated lessons orally out loud, to imprint the words upon our memory. Arithmetic tables, poems and little rhymes about the days of the week and months of the year were also included. Rote it and note it, seemed to be our task.

Books and pencils, due to the high cost of paper, were only for the teacher. Children had slates and chalk. We were, however, taught the value of being able to write letters neatly and clearly, in a 'copperplate' style. How it appeared on our slates varied widely, but I enjoyed this.

I was also more delighted than most to be selected for the school choir, and excitedly joined the others in the hall where 'we selected few' were to be given a well-known piece to sing in unison. As this was a special occasion I even took off my white rubber collar, gave it a quick spit and rub with a hanky to clean it, and put it back on.

We were lined up in two rows and told what to sing. The master conducted, but was clearly not content with the overall quality of our output. He walked slowly along the line with an ear cocked sideways, in order to sample more closely the individual sounds making up the harmonious blend.

He stopped at me, turned his head outwards and paused with his ear in my direction for thirty or more seconds. "Harry," he said sadly, shaking his head, "Go and report to Mr Seaton and ask if you can please join his lesson until we have finished." He was quite obviously trying to tell me something, and I had cleaned my collar for nothing.

In 1904 we lost another schoolboy hero 'Sir H.M.Stanley' who died at his home in London. Who hadn't heard of this Welshman from Denbigh and his epic journey to find Dr. Livingstone in Africa? A great traveller and adventurer, latterly he had been elected Liberal-Democrat MP for North Lambeth.

So it progressed, there were so many interesting stories month by month. Nothing we could take part in of course, but something in which we could take pride. It added to our Nation and to our British Empire, but in between the proud and the glorious, would be the odd report like the 1904 Baltic outrage, in which the Hull fishing fleet had been fired upon by Russian warships off Dogger Bank. The trawler Crano was sunk, two men killed and six more injured. No one seemed to fully understand the reasons for it!

By 1909 there were many complaints about the horse drawn carriages being driven too fast by the cabbies in the city. The dangerous driving and the overcrowded roads were almost impossible to cross. The problems also of the smell and discomfort, from so much manure being splashed, spread and trodden in.

Much of this was presented in 'News Headlines.' Other reports centred upon prophecy such as "Doom of the Hansom" suggesting that the Hansom carriages would be replaced by the speedy 'motor-cabs.' This bold theory must have been loudly accentuated as a sure sign of the future, when, at the Olympia Motor Show of that year, on stand number 87, the Model T Ford, a 20 hp touring Phaeton, was introduced.

Of greater interest to me however at 14 years old, was the new game, sold in 'sets' and called a 'Jigsaw' puzzle game. Priced from one shilling with eighty pieces, up to two guineas with one thousand pieces, it would be many years before I could have one.

There were two major events in 1910. His Majesty King Edward VII died. Our new monarch became His Majesty King George V. This was the third monarch in my life and I was still only coming on fifteen years old.

The second major event was ours. Having outgrown the present one, we moved to another house in Aberdeen Street, Winson Green. Moving was quite usual and houses were no problem to find. The only difficulty was finding the money to pay the rent each week when the rent man called. The size of working family therefore governed the size of house. It was at this time I met Freddy Hill, who was to become a very close friend. He also lived in Aberdeen Street. We got along fine and were inseparable. I was just a little older, but Fred and I developed similar interests as time went by.

Mitchell's & Butlers Ltd, the Birmingham brewers at Cape Hill, held the Queens Head in Aberdeen Street. My father, being the oldest member of the Queens Head Cycling Club and a very keen touring cyclist, wanted me to join as well as all my brothers, though not old enough to go into the pub, I nevertheless joined the club, we then represented the oldest and the youngest members, which pleased him greatly.

Most pubs had clubs of one sort or another. It was a way of attracting custom and generating loyalty. There were bowling, darts, cycling and fishing clubs or teams, with matches and competitions at home and away. Many had funds for 'Sick and Dividend' societies from which the out-of-work customers could draw ready cash if an illness struck.

The pubs were a very useful part of the social structure, as well as recreation. Cycle club outings were most enjoyable and I went on many of them. My bike was second or third hand however, and as I got older, I preferred to go out with Freddy rather than dear old dad.

Once starting work and earning money, Fred and I decided to join the Birchfield Harriers Sports Club. Fred's father Eli, a cycle maker and dealer with a small shop on the Spring Hill, was himself an ex-racer and was delighted by this, so delighted that he made us each a racing bike (at knock down prices).

The machines were lightweight, with cane rims and no lever or cable brakes, ideal for racing and we did well. The bikes could only be slowed down or restrained, by means of the fixed rear wheel and leg power. One day, a potentially dangerous disadvantage of this, became obvious to me. After

Members of the 'Queens Head' Aberdeen Street, Cycle Club, well supported by the Morgan family.
back row, left with cycle - Walter. sixth from left - Jack. seventh from left - Joe.
middle row seated, third from left - Frank. fifth from left - Fred.
front row, second from left (Father) Arthur, third from left - Our Harry.

work, most evenings, we went for training rides and on one of these occasions, I was merrily powering out towards Stourport, where some of my father's relatives still lived. At one point of this journey was a very steep downward descent, known as Mucklows Hill.

Knowing this to be a twisting, winding, nightmare if taken too fast, I heavily back pressured the pedals against the rear hub sprocket. It was too much to take, and the chain snapped.

My life flashed before me at each bend and I felt that I had broken every land speed record in existence. I hung on, but it frightened me to death. Father had no sympathy however, and later on when I told him all about it, his only reply was "Oi ave no toim for they new fangled machines."

As I got older, my father and I seemed to mildly clash on more frequent occasions. I think perhaps I was starting to get a little dissatisfied with my life and my future, or lack of it. Brothers and sisters were leaving to get married and start families. There was also some talk at this time, about disturbances in Europe.

The Baltic countries were often in the news. Not that I knew where the Baltic countries were, or who lived in them, I took very little interest, as there was no chance of me ever leaving England. Holidays to us simply meant not having to go to work. Other countries were simply names in books, and even visiting other towns in England was a rarity for the working class, so my interest was not aroused.

Talk was now turning to the possibility of a war in Europe. Unusual experiments were being carried out, like the ones enabling pilots to drop bombs from the air, and in 1912 the War Office announced the building of a new 'Flying Corps', with HQ on Salisbury Plain. This plan allowed for the purchase of 131 new aeroplanes. It was also revealed in an International report that France planned to build 344 new aeroplanes, Russia 300, Germany? Not known.

Our own country meanwhile was not without excitement. The problems in Ireland, with its conflict between Protestant/Catholic plus North/South & IRA confrontations, appeared to be irreconcilable.

The Women's Social and Political Union, a well-supported group of Suffragists, founded by Mrs Emmeline Pankhurst on 10 October 1903, was continuously, and now ferociously, active in the quest for equal Parliamentary votes for women.

One morning at about 6am, on 19 February 1913, there was an explosion at a new 14 room house, overlooking Walton Heath golf course. Building cost had been around £2000, a high figure for that period. Neighbours rushed to the scene and it was later determined, that fourteen pounds of gunpowder had been used, in an attempt to demolish it.

At a meeting in Cardiff that night, Mrs Pankhurst was reported as saying: "We have blown up the Chancellor of the Exchequer's house." When asked why, her reply was, "To wake him up."

Some four months after this, on 4 June 1913, Emily Wilding Davison ran onto the Epsom racecourse during the Derby meeting, and fell beneath the hooves of 'Anmer' the Kings horse. She died four days later.

Back on the European front, at the end of June 1914, from Sarajevo, Bosnia, news came of the assassination of the Archduke Francis Ferdinand and his wife, the Duchess of Hohenberg. Having escaped the explosion from the first bomb thrown at their vehicle, the couple were later on their way, to pay a hospital visit and meet those members of the crowd injured by it, when a second bomb was directed at them. This did not explode, but a Servian youth fired an automatic pistol at the couple, wounding them seriously enough to result in their death a short time later.

A local conflict resulted from this event, between Austria-Hungary and Serbia on 28 July 1914. Shortly afterwards, Germany declared war on Russia, Saturday 1 August 1914. Germany then attacked France, without any declaration of war, making an assault at three points, Longwy, Cirey and Delle, and advanced into Luxembourg.

There existed at that time, a law of Europe and a Treaty of London, between Britain, France and Germany, with an 'Amendment-Appendix' signed on 19 April 1839 in London. This guaranteed the neutrality of Belgium and, when Germany went into that neutral State, it violated the agreement, presenting a direct challenge to Gt. Britain, who sent a warning to Germany, to the effect that if they set foot in Belgium, the British Navy would take appropriate action.

It was now fairly obvious to all, that this situation had become dangerous. In the meantime Germany demanded Belgium to allow her troops through their territory. Belgium refused and the King of the Belgians requested aid from King George. The House of Commons made a statement that we would:-

1 'Defend the French coast against German Naval attack.'
2 'Protect Belgian neutrality if violated by Germany.'
3 'Use all our forces.'

Germany refused to give any assurances for respect of neutrality and, as they were already in Luxembourg; at 11.00 p.m. on 4 August 1914, came the official declaration of war between Gt. Britain and Germany. Mobilisation for the British army began, Reserves were called and a Territorial force created.

'WE WERE AT WAR'

(Music Hall recruitment song)

The army and the navy need attention,
The outlook isn't healthy you'll admit
But I've a perfect dream, of a new recruiting scheme
which I think, is absolutely it.

If all the other girls would do as I do,
I believe that we could manage it alone,
For I turn all suitors from me,
but the Sailor and the Tommy,
I've a Navy and an Army of my own.

******

On Sunday I walk out with a Soldier,
Monday, I'm taken by a Tar.
On Tuesday I'm out, with a baby boy Scout,
On Wednesday a Hussar
On Thursday I gang oot wi a Scotty
On Friday the Captain of the Crew,
And on Saturday I'm willing, - if you'll only take the shilling
To make a man of any one of you!.

Two

British Expeditionary Force

By 1913 England was a country in doubt, fearful at the thought of war, yet excited by patriotism. This situation was then exploited by the combined powerful, political and financial forces of the Government, Press and Industry. It reached a head in 1914 when men were actively and openly encouraged to 'join up' to help create a "British Expeditionary Force." (B.E.F). Bands played in the streets, to give a military flavour. This was all voluntary, with no conscription at this time.

Women rushed by the million to enter into war work. The Union Jack was seen everywhere. Some over-keen girls, pushed white feathers into the hands of those young men, not seen to be 'answering the call.' Many newspapers published the Recruiting Song and most Music Halls presented it as a 'set piece.'

"Your King and Country Need You:"

We watched you playing cricket and every kind of game
At football Golf and Polo you may have made your name
But now your Country calls you, to play your part in war
And no matter what befalls you, we shall love you all the more
So come and join the Forces as your Fathers did before;

Oh - we don't want to lose you, but we think you ought to go
For your King and your Country both need you so,
We shall want you and miss you but with all our might and main
We shall cheer you, thank you, kiss you, when you come home again.

Posters in abundance carried statements to shame or disgrace anyone not joining up, like the one carrying the words "Why are you stopping here when your pals are out there?"(Dec.1914) or "Think! Are you content for him to fight for you?"

The illustration of Field Marshal Lord Kitchener with his finger grimly pointing at all who passed, bore the simple words - "Your Country Needs - YOU." It became universally the most famous of posters. It was all that was necessary, as at that time, he was possibly the most famous man in the land. He had recaptured Khartoum from the Muslims, and served as C.I.C in India. He was also the first serving officer to hold the post of Secretary of State for War in Asquith's cabinet 5 August 1914, and he had made a great effort, to expand the British army. Regrettably, he drowned on 5 June 1916 when the cruiser 'Hampshire' taking him to Russia, struck a mine. He was, I think, the only outstanding military figure on either side to meet a violent end.

During the latter months of 1913, Freddy and I had many chats about the prospect of travel and we both felt that if we joined up, we would have an exciting time. It was when two of my brothers volunteered for the army that I was spurred into making a radical change to my life, and happily Fred was in full agreement.

With those married having left home, another move was now made necessary to a smaller house in Winson Green, 150 'little' Peel Street, the next street up from Aberdeen Street. It was called 'little' Peel St. because of a larger continuation of it over an intersecting road, inspiringly known as 'big' Peel Street.

Many members of the family lived there with their children. Our end of the street was a cul-de-sac, blocked at one end by the massive 12 foot high boundary wall of the Dudley Road hospital grounds. There was no doubt that my life was getting emptier, so together with Fred, the decision was made.

We both went to sign on, in early October 1913 still seventeen years old, having been caught up in the general excitement. To us, it appeared a rare opportunity, so, we jointly agreed, after many serious discussions on the subject, that we would go to the recruiting office in Birmingham, and join the Hussars. Without a doubt, that was the most colourful and decorative uniform we had seen. It would certainly appeal to the girls, and what a dash we would cut, in those tight trousers and braided jackets, imagine the fun coming home on leave in such a rich and resplendent uniform!

The recruiting sergeant was most understanding but not too sure that we were old enough to join any regiment.

"Walk around the block lads, think about it," he suggested, "Then come back, and by the time you return, I wouldn't be at all surprised if you were nearer the right age!" So, we walked slowly around the block discussing the implications and our great disappointment.

"What do you think he meant Harry?" Asked Fred.

"Well; I think he wanted to take us" I replied "But perhaps he is not allowed to, if we are under eighteen."

"Is eighteen the acceptable age then?" Fred asked,

"I don't know, but it seems to be for most things," was all I could say.

"Then let's go back in and use different birth dates and make ourselves a year older," Fred suggested.

So that was what we did. Once around the block and back into the recruitment office. There, we added a year to our previously stated ages and it was just as the sergeant had predicted, we were both now old enough to join.

"Welcome lads, you're just the sort of keen young chaps we are looking for. Unfortunately, you're not quite the required height for the Hussars: However, there is another noble regiment, with very similar prestige and just as many long-standing battle honours. A regiment proudly boasting service in the reign of Elizabeth and in the Dutch service from 1674 to 1688. It became famous as The Sixth Foot. Fought bravely with the Prince of Orange in 1678, returned in 1685 to deal with the Duke of Monmouth's rebellion.

They have served in theatres of war all over the world, France, Spain, Jamaica, and the West Indies. With only six hundred men, they captured Minorca, 2 September 1705. Sadly the British lost it again shortly after, but what a marvellous effort eh- lads? The regiment was finally renamed, after the county most of its men came from."

He carried on with this stream of information, sometimes standing still, but mostly pacing the short distance back and forth behind his tiny desk, looking alternately at us, the ceiling and the floor, bringing us right up to date with the Regiments' service in India and all sorts of exciting places that were magical names to both of us. It sounded just what we wanted and we were delighted to accept. That was how Freddy and I came to take the 'King's Shilling' and join the Royal Warwickshire Regiment!

After a considerable wait, we both received notice of our initial training course and in February 1914, we received our call to Budbrooke barracks in Warwick, for a period of five months 'Special Reserve Training' (SRT). It was an adventure, it was exciting and I loved every minute. Once that was over however, it was back home again in July and life was once more getting rather dreary.

Eventually, an even more exciting event than the training course had arrived. Never shall I forget the day I received my mobilisation papers. I was just about the proudest chap alive. Eighteen and a half years old, knowing nothing of war and its horrors, brim full of eager anticipation and excitement, yearning for the day I would rejoin my battalion. My day was 8 August 1914, but I couldn't resist going to see-off the Section "D" men, leaving for their various regiments on 5 of August.

It is quite impossible for me to explain the thrill experienced as I watched them, with wives, mothers, and sweethearts, dancing and singing with them along the roads. People cheering and waving Union Jacks, joy and jubilation abounding.

The swelling pride was infectious. Bottles of scotch were much in evidence at the railway station, with all manner of toasts direct from the bottle, mainly the toast for a speedy and victorious return. There was no doubt whatsoever that each person on that railway platform expected the war with Germany to end in our favour within six months. It was quite remarkable and yet it was a nation-wide belief. Perhaps it was started by a shrewd rumour, purposely spread by our own propaganda agencies, whoever they were and wherever they might have been. After all, people would be a lot keener to go to war for a short time, rather than a long one.

The train entered the station slowly, approaching the buffers with caution. It gave out a mighty blast of steam and came to rest in a moist white cloud, which, gradually dispersing, revealed once more the happy faces of the intended passengers. Soldiers took their places in an orderly part-trained manner, they bade farewell, kisses were reached for, and doors were closed. Railway staff traversed the train checking door handles for the locked position.

The Guard stepped from his rear van, looked at his watch, eyed the signal, waved his green flag, blew two shrill, alternating blasts on his whistle and the train moved out as he was stepping back onboard: Then they were all gone, fading into the distance: Most of them forever!

What they did NOT see, as they departed for the front line, were their once cheering loved ones, now in the throes of extreme remorse. All were heartbroken, some hysterical, many unable to leave the station for a considerable time. They had very bravely held this back until now.

So how did this affect me? Not a bit, how could I know the feelings of a father leaving his wife and children, or the feelings of a wife sending off her man to the battle front, not knowing if they would ever meet again.

I was single, without a care in the world, what did it matter to me? It simply meant a new exciting experience, like nothing I had known before. It was great, it was going to be fun, I was so very much looking forward to it. I was eighteen and a half and a dreamer, with such a lot to learn.

tune of - (Oh- I do like to be beside the Seaside)

Oh, I do like to see a lot of Soldiers
Soldiers are what I like to see
And if they have a sort of horse
Then I like them more of course
Because I just love, the Cavalry

Three

The Draft

8 August 1914

At long last, the 8 August came around. I visited all my brothers and sisters, who still lived in the Winson Green district even though, by now, most of them were married. Families very rarely scattered or moved away from their roots. Jack and Walter had already left for the Army and Frank was preparing to leave. Fred and I were the only boys now living with our parents, at the new home in Peel Street. I also called in to see Liz, my girlfriend who lived with her parents at number 2 back of 30, Stour Street, Spring Hill.

We had known each other for a long time through childhood, nothing serious, but she said she would miss me; and that was nice. We agreed to write regularly, though I could never have guessed how difficult that would be for me to do later on. Our goodbyes completed, I called at the Hills' house, 4 Carlton Place, Aberdeen Street, to collect my pal Fred. After saying goodbye to Eli and Sarah, his Mum and Dad, together we went to join the assembly and be led through the cheering crowds.

The waving flags, the shouts of joy, all the way to Snow Hill rail station. How did I feel now? How did we both feel? We swelled with pride, good God, we were soldiers going to join our regiments, and off to win a war.

What young folk of our age could help but be thrilled, with all these people wishing us well, cheering us on, slapping us on the back. It was most exciting and flattering. As the train steamed out of the station, we felt a sense of achievement already and we hadn't yet begun.

Reaching the town of Warwick, the group became fragmented and began straggling along the road towards Budbrooke barracks. Some of the older soldiers called at the various public houses on the way, although a few of them had already tanked up in Birmingham and on the train journey. Freddy and I, like the keen soldiers we were, went direct to the barracks and reported to the Guardroom, to hand in our papers.

The barracks were vastly different now to the way they were during our initial peacetime training period here. Where once spotless, orderly, bright and polished, it was now untidy, all bustle and excitement like a market place on Saturday night. Colour sergeants demonstrating the power of their lungs and officers anxiously awaiting the men to be sorted out.

Regimental numbers were called, and our new clothing, with equipment, thrown at us. All barrack rooms were full of men changing into uniform. One of us enquired, "Where can we change sergeant?"

"Go outside and change on the square, plenty of space out there lad," he bellowed. We went out and joined many others. So, out there on the parade ground we peeled off our civilian clothing, underclothing as well, until we were stark naked.

I glanced over towards the 'Married' quarters where the women were watching us from their windows. The smiles and laughter on their faces said it all. It would have been interesting to have overheard their remarks, I can well imagine what some of the comment might have been, and we would probably have had more than just a few moments of sheer embarrassment, had we been able to listen in. I tended to rather shyly melt into the crowd at first, but eventually, mixing with some of the older warriors, that tendency disappeared. After all it is quite easy to hide in a crowd.

We were now back in uniform and feeling like soldiers:

"FALL IN." We lined up, Freddy at my side. We were now officially 1553 Private Morgan and 1554 Private Hill. Lumps of bread and cheese were handed to us, which we shoved into our haversacks to be eaten later. Eventually, the arrival of our captain, who would take us on to the Isle of Wight, signalled action. He moved to the head of the column, the commands were given, a drum beat out the step, and the band joined in. Now we were on the move, through the gates and down the road towards Warwick.

It was marvellous to swing along with the lads again, to be amongst their cheery chatter and jokes. It really is impossible to describe the feeling of marching behind a military band, to someone who has never had that experience. Children found it difficult to resist and many joined us for short distances. It was no wonder that the 'Pied Piper' got away with it as he did, but added to this, was the special occasion that it represented, which made it extra enjoyable.

Freddy and I continuously looked at each other and grinned. We were as happy as two small children on a day out. When we reached Warwick, crowds of people lined the streets, more cheering and waving of flags, all the way through the town. It was wonderful! They probably all thought that we were going straight off to France. Whatever they thought didn't really matter. It suited the younger ones of us, to have such a tremendous fuss made. In fact we had already won the war, at least we felt as if we had.

A train carried us from Warwick to Southampton, where we boarded the Ferry to the Isle of Wight and in no time at all, we arrived at Newport. From there we marched to our camp, some two miles distant, where we went under canvas next door to Parkhurst prison, with some exceptionally hard training in front of us. In grand weather, strong tents, in the fresh, sweet air, plenty of good food and exercise, we were soon in the pink of condition and ready for anything.

It was during this initial period that I almost made a dreadful error through a totally innocent misunderstanding. We were gathered in a large hall for some administrational purpose and were called to a table at the front of the assembly. An officer with two corporals and a sergeant sat there passing forms to and fro and writing in various books. One by one we were called out, and asked questions to ascertain next of kin and the like.

When my turn came, I went forward and the officer began the interview by asking many questions, which resulted in the others at the table adding ticks, circles or crosses to their respective schedules without looking up. He then advised me, that as I had a mother at home, who still had a family to look after, I had an option to send her part of my army pay to help out.

"How much of it would you like to contribute?" he asked.

"All of it sir," I said.

At this, everyone at the table stopped writing and all heads were raised.

"All of it?" He questioned

"All of it sir," I confirmed.

The officer pushed his chair back, and stood to address the assembly.

"I have a young man here, who is prepared to make an inspirational gesture. He is offering to provide as a gift, the whole of his service pay to his dear mother, to help her raise those members of his family still at home. This is indeed a commendable acknowledgement of love and appreciation, and his mother can be proud of him, it sets an example to us all; but I cannot allow it."

Pulling his chair forward once more to the table, he sat down, saying to the sergeant as he did so,

'Our Harry' seated left, with Freddy Hill standing. Taken by Haward Studio, High Street, Newport, I.o.W, shortly after being 'kitted out' for training and France.

"Quite touching, really touching sergeant" the sergeant nodded in agreement. Then to me he said

"I cannot possibly let you make such a sacrifice, and I suggest you make a donation from your one shilling a day, of about three pence a day which I am sure she will appreciate.

I agreed and he stood once more, reached out to shake my hand, after which I took a step back, saluted, turned right and moved smartly away. I could not get out of there quickly enough! Such an embarrassment, because what he and the others didn't know was that although they were talking of a permanent donation for the rest of my service, I thought the donation was just for the first WEEK only!

As the days went by, I grew increasingly restless and impatient saying to Fred, "What if the war is over before we get there mate? We won't see anything and we will lose our chance. Some of those who have already gone, came here to the I.o.W. after us."

"Never mind Harry" he said, "It won't be long before we go, and I am sure we will see some of it, at least."

But I felt badly about the delay and felt that something could surely be done to speed up the slowness of the system, so that we could go. I had waited so long for this chance to go abroad and here we were wasting valuable time. Though I did not think Fred was nearly as concerned about the problem as I was. He seemed to be perfectly content to let the rota work it's own way down to us.

Oh- Belgium put the Kibosh on the Kaiser
Europe took a stick and made him sore
On his throne it hurts to sit
And when John Bull starts to hit
He will never sit upon it any more

He'll have to go to school again and learn his geography
He quite forgot Britannia and the hands across the sea
Australia, and Canada, the Russian and the Jap
And England looked so small he couldn't see her on the map.

Oh- Belgium put the Kibosh on the Kaiser
Europe took a stick and made him sore
She should shout with victory joy
Hold your hand out naughty boy
You must never play at soldiers any more.

Four

Machine Gun Training

September 1914

It was now September 1914 and I decided to see the sergeant major about some action. He was not particularly sympathetic however, and his advice was simply put, "Rest contented where you are lad, there are no bullets flying around this camp. Just appreciate what you've got and control your anxiety, you'll be in the thick of it, all in good time!" So, for now, I had to be content and leave it at that.

Our daily training was becoming monotonous, so I requested a transfer to the Machine Gun Section. What a pleasant surprise I had when the request was granted. On the appropriate day I reported to an armourer sergeant along with several other trainees.

We were seated in a semicircle around him, whilst he stood in the centre of the arc beside a seriously businesslike tripod-mounted machine gun. It appeared to have taken root into the floorboards so solid did it look. He eyed us each in turn and said;

"You will either one day be pleased to have taken this course, or will one day regret it. But whatever that turns out to be, you will know all there is to know about the weapons we are covering on this course and where they will one day fit into a totally revised military strategy."

"This," he continued, "is a Vickers Machine Gun developed from the Vickers Maxim, which was modified to reduce the weight to forty pounds. The new Gun also has a much improved mechanism." Our interest developed to fascination as he described the action of the unit, pausing briefly to rob the machine of certain parts, with the dexterity of a pickpocket.

He tapped the barrel lightly with a finger before caressing it lovingly with the palm of his hand, as he went on. "The barrel is water cooled by a surrounding metal sleeve or jacket." With hardly a pause he suddenly stopped and pointed at one member of the class, asking

"You, soldier, how do we keep the barrel cool?"

"With water sergeant" the lad replied.

"Where from?"

"From a tap?" The lad asked in response.

"I ask the questions, you give the answers: All right?" The sergeant said.

"All right sergeant; - er, from a tap!"

The sergeant walked slowly around the formidable weapon in two full circles, muttering quietly, but audibly,

"From a tap; from a tap; from a tap." He stopped to face us all, looked studiously at the floor, raised his head slowly to scan the whole group then met the gaze of his victim. "My dear young man, by the time you have been where you are all going," his voice began to get louder as he finished the sentence, "After a few months, you will have forgotten entirely **what a tap looks like!** You will collect water from anywhere that you see it, from rain filled water holes, upturned steel helmets, water bottles taken from enemy bodies, tea cans, water rations, your friends' water rations, anybody's water rations and if all this fails," he stopped, stepped forward and leaned down towards the lad, then practically with noses touching he quietly said, "YOU WILL PISS IN IT! What you will *not do* is leave the jacket without Coolant. "Now, lad," standing upright again, "What do you do?"

"Piss in it sergeant!"

"Right! Good. But don't get too close, because it gets bloody hot and YOU-WILL-WELD."

He knew from our laughter that he now had our full attention and carried on.

"The Gun is recoil operated and accepts seven pints of water around the barrel. It fires .303 ammunition, the same as your Lee Enfield rifles. We feed it from a webbing fabric belt holding 250 cartridges and in return for your diligent care and attention, it will fire 450 rounds every minute.

Slow, when compared to some others maybe, but this will still be firing at the enemy when the others have stopped. It has a slight disadvantage in that, a barrel will only fire ten thousand rounds, which would be about one hour of continuous firing, after which you will need to change the barrel. You will be taught how to do that. However, remember it will be much easier to change a barrel here, but not quite so easy when rows and rows of nasty Germans are advancing at you.

Any questions?"

"Yes Sergeant," a hand was raised, "Seven pints is rather a long piss and I don't think I could manage it." The sergeant let the laughter fade.

"Right! That's fair comment. In that event, you will take a collecting tin to all your mates and find out who your real friends are! However, on a serious note, it is unlikely you will boil the jacket dry, just remember we are talking here of life or death, your life, or your death, and you will see no humour in that. Be well aware of the need and check the level frequently."

Each day we attended, the course revealed more about the Vickers and the Lewis guns. We were taught how to strip and clean them, oil and reassemble, in daylight and blindfolded. I felt a closer affinity towards the Lewis Gun, simply because it was made by the Birmingham Small Arms Company (B.S.A) in my home town.

The sergeant was an easy man to talk to and we learned fast. On the last day of training, he sadly admitted,

"Although you are now well trained on the Vickers, it is unlikely that all of you will have a chance to put that training into practice. I can say, that initially only two Vickers machine guns will be supplied to each **battalion** of Infantry.

They are in extremely short supply at the present time, and to my regret," he confided, "The British Army does not yet appreciate fully, the superior fire power of the weapon, which is why no move has yet been made to create a Machine Gun Corps. For your sakes, I hope we accept the changing situation before the Germans do, otherwise our cavalry are in for an uncomfortably rough ride, and you chaps will be severely disadvantaged."

A most enjoyable course reached its conclusion and I was absolutely delighted to be passed-out, 'Machine Gunner First Class.' However, I could not help thinking about his comments. I thought that everyone in the army knew fully the requirements of going to war, yet if I understood him correctly the people making the decisions are not at the front line, and did not see the importance of machine guns.

My younger brother Fred intended joining up as soon as he could, and he was keen on the cavalry. That would be all six of us in a front line posting somewhere in Europe. It was something of a frightening thought that these major weapons, could perhaps not even be under consideration!

We were now into the first few days of October. Outside, I found a number of chaps from my unit clustered around the Daily Order Board. It displayed a list of NCOs and men on the next draft for France.

My heart sank when I scanned it and failed yet again to find my name. If only I had known about the actuality of war, as did some of the old soldiers around me, what a different reaction the omission of my name would have produced. "Forget it Harry," they said "Let it drift!" You will go out in good time and then be pleased to come back, take advantage of the peace and quiet while you have it, with the washing facility, canteen, warm bed and life, you won't be seeing any of that in Belgium or France."

They did not feel my anger and frustration, they were trying to comfort me but I refused to be comforted or put off my intent. In a sudden burst of pent up emotion, I rushed straight to the sergeant major's tent to curse him, openly, man to man.

I shall never know how I missed being put on a charge, or how he kept his temper under control. What an idiot he must have thought me to be. He was obviously an extremely understanding and tolerant man, remaining unruffled as he sternly rebuked my approach and explained in no uncertain terms what he could have done with me. Under the circumstances, he ended his lecture with these words, "This scrap will go on for some years yet my lad, but just for your bloody cheek, I shall stick you on the next draft."

He was a man of his word. On 9 October 1914 another list was posted and my name was up there for all to see. I was joining the First Battalion R.War.R. My elation at being able to write home to my family and Liz, to say I was now off to France, was indescribable. I had to say, "By the time you receive this letter I will have gone!"

The message was at once big, brave and mighty, I felt all these things. Pride wrongly placed, can be a gigantic conceit, such was my ignorance. I noticed a different attitude altogether in Freddy, he was unusually quiet.

"Does that mean we now split up" he asked.

"Well, I suppose it does for a short time, as your name is not on the list," I replied,

"But as soon as you come over we can meet up again, at least we know we are both going to France and will both be with the Warwick's."

I must admit, this situation had never occurred to me. Sadly, because of my forceful request, he was now not on my draft and would have to wait. Perhaps things would have been different, had I not compelled the sergeant major to act out of sequence, who knows. I just did not stop to think!

Whatever the circumstance, we were destined to separate and our paths would now go in two different directions, from this point on. At the time, this did not seem so important. Having never been to France or Belgium, we had no idea of the size of each country. I could calmly say, "See you over there" with no conception of circumstance or distance.

Comrades, comrades, ever since we were boys,
Sharing each others sorrows, sharing each others joys.

26

Five

Departure

11 October 1914

On 11 October 1914, we paraded on the square ready for the big adventure. Standing in the ranks, I looked around for Fred. He was just behind me looking terribly downcast and miserable. I simply had to break ranks and go over to him. I took his right hand with both of mine, saying "So long 1554, don't worry mate, I'll see you over there."

A high pitched scream vibrated over the parade ground from the direction of the officer "What the hell do you think you are doing soldier, get back into ranks immediately." It seemed to me more important to say goodbye to Fred at that particular time, than to be concerned about straight lines, however, one more hand squeeze and I moved quickly back to my place.

The regimental band had now lined up. An order followed **"Form Fours, Right, By the Right, Quick March"** - and to the tune of 'The Warwickshire Lads and Lassies,' we started on the journey I had craved for since mobilisation day. Smiling, I turned my head to look at Fred and gave him a reassuring wink. I saw his face, his expression. Never, as long as I live, would I forget the sadness in his eyes. A look of absolute and utter misery. It was a considerable time after that, before I was able to manage a smile, his image haunted me and was etched upon my memory.

The gates leading from the square, as well as the main roads from the camp, were crowded with people giving us a warm send-off. The band was striving to make itself heard over the noise and the combination was electrifying. We marched to Cowes where the local folk threw cigarettes, pipes, matches and chocolates, from their bedroom windows.

I was not fast enough in the scramble to make any great gains and retrieved more bruises than cigarettes. Soon we were boarding the boat and leaving the port, most of us remained at the side rail where we watched and waved to the gathered crowd on the pier.

My attention however was finally settled on the band, now playing the somewhat emotional tune of Auld Lang Syne. As the distance between us increased, the sound became thinner, "Should auld acquaintance be forgot and never brought to mind" drifted across the quiet still waters and a chill ran down my spine.

I thought of my brothers and 1554 Fred, I knew nothing was for certain but surely we would all be OK! I wondered how many of us onboard would make the return journey. As long as the band was still audible, every man on that boat was silent. We were half way to Southampton before the sound died away completely

Arriving at Southampton we embarked on a large transport vessel for the journey to France. Named "The Australind," it was not just a cattle ship, but a filthy cattle ship. Surely someone could have hosed it down first. Were we really so desperate? I shall never forget that sailing. There was no place free of cow shit, so sitting or resting was right out of the question. We all stayed on deck and watched England fade into the distance.

I glanced around at my fellow passengers wondering what was going through their minds at that moment. The older men who had left wives and children, all looked worried and sad. I had to admit a dislike for standing in cow shit, but honestly I had no worries additional to that. Had I not been looking forward to this day and longing for it to arrive? I tried to convince myself that this mode of transport was no reflection on the way our country calculated our value!

Quite close to us in the channel, were three battle cruisers in escort. What a fine and stirring sight they were, ploughing through the water which curled up on each side of their bows, like white frothy lapels. Their crews busily engaged in sending and receiving a constant flow of visual signals to each other.

A shout broke the silence when some of our lads sighted the French coast. I could see it too and from that moment, I never lifted my eyes from it. Nearer and nearer it came until we could see the docks of Le Havre, lined with French citizens. As this was in the early part of the war, the arrival of English troops in France was a new happening. It was a big event for them, and an even bigger event for me. I was at last going to another country, and would actually be in France!

The German army was now making rapid advancement towards Paris, with little opposition, so the excitement of the French people was considerable when they saw the arrival of our ship. Not an impressive entrance to make however, as it is extremely difficult to look, or feel, like a heroic figure, arriving in a shit caked cattle carrier, but nevertheless, they were delighted to see us.

We tied up amidst their rousing cheers and gave out with our own cry of "Vive la France." After that we were lined up and went flat out to show the onlookers how smartly we could right dress, number, form fours and march off. That was our intention, but we were suddenly, excitedly, attacked by them all, particularly the women and girls who threw their arms around our necks, hugging us and kissing our cheeks. Terrible, it was! Such rare suffering for young Englishmen. We faced up to it resolutely however, and enjoyed it to the full.

My luck appeared to be on the wane at first and I found myself in the arms of a rough looking Frenchman in his sixties, whilst the chap on my right had a young girl on each shoulder, having a field day. I hated him, but couldn't bear to see anyone being so outnumbered, and so shamefully taken advantage of in a strange land, so I shook off my old boy politely, and helped a colleague out of his distress! Was this what the war was going to be like? I loved it!

The French people were most kind. We were given cigarettes, fruit, bread, cheese, in fact my haversack was stuffed full of all sorts of produce. On the march to the camp I was able to start eating some of it, to lighten the load. There were to be many such marches as this in the future, but sadly not all would be so pleasant.

After a good nights sleep, we started training again at eight o'clock in the morning. This became the pattern for several days, when suddenly we were needed for reinforcement to the First Battalion, Royal Warwickshire Regiment. They were part of the Tenth Infantry Brigade and had been in action. We were now urgently needed to fill the gaps left by their killed and wounded.

Immediately, we were rushed aboard a cattle train, (couldn't they find any other form of transport for us?) and started our journey to the front line. Each railway truck held about forty men. We never reached a higher speed than ten miles an hour, and made frequent stops for periods of about 15 minutes each time, no one had the slightest idea why.

At these stops, the troops would dash up to the engine and ask the driver to fill their canteens with water from his boiler, so that they could make tea. He did so, for a time, but then appeared to tire of it and refused, with a lot of arm waving and a great deal of French language. It was perhaps good for everyone that he could not be understood! That way no one became too upset.

Finally, we arrived at a tiny place called La Crêche, just a few miles south east of Bailleul, where we were taken to a barn. There, we waited for the First Battalion, to be relieved out of the trenches by the Dublin Fusiliers, who were also with the Tenth Bde. When they arrived, the draft men naturally turned out to see them, for these were the remains of what Kaiser Bill scathingly called 'Britain's Contemptible Little Army.' known thereafter to the troops as simply, 'The Old Contemptibles', a tag that was used affectionately by many and accepted proudly by these experienced men, many of whom had been through previous conflicts.

The soldiers of the British army at this time consisted of 'all regulars', we were mostly 'new boys.' It was a strange situation with the British regular army. Before the war, the public had a low opinion of them. They supposedly had no homes and were variously idle, roguish, or orphaned. Now of course, the situation was rapidly changing. They were needed and their image had miraculously improved.

Britain's fickle population held a new viewpoint concerning these 150,000 men (six infantry and one cavalry, divisions), of the Expeditionary Corps, who had already helped to save Paris, just a few months ago, with delaying actions at Mons and Le Câteau.

After the withdrawal from Mons, on 23 August 1914 during these 'Battles of the Frontiers,' Sir John French, commander of BEF ordered a retreat south west. The German First Army was close on its heels and had almost caught up with BEF II Corps (Gen. Horace Smith-Dorrien) by the time they reached Le Câteau, (35 miles from Mons and 18 miles north of St.Quentin).

It was then realised that BEF I Corps (Lt.Gen.Douglas Haig) was some 12 miles further away, beyond the Forest of Mormal. So, on the 26 August 1914, Smith-Dorrien decided that his men would be overpowered if they continued to retreat and Sir John French's order was disobeyed. BEF II Corps stood and fought a delaying action. Three and a half British divisions engaged the full strength of the German First Army, which was twice their size, in men and artillery.

The encounter lasted eleven hours and it was said that not since Waterloo had the British army fought such a battle. By nightfall, they disengaged and continued the retreat in the direction of St Quentin. There was no meaningful pursuit by the enemy who had suffered heavy losses. British losses were 8,000 men and 38 guns, from a total of 40,000 men.

Even now at this particular moment in time, their comrades were making a marvellous stand at Ypres. Outnumbered by ten to one, they were immovable and earned a reputation second to none. As I watched the men of the First battalion, I felt so proud of them. Proud of their achievements and prouder still that I had been granted the privilege to join their Ranks.

Being now a part of the Fourth Infantry Division, commanded by Brig. Gen. J.A.L. Haldane CB.DSO. Our GOC being Brig.Gen. T.D. O'Snow CB. The full attachment of our Unit in The Tenth Infantry Brigade was:-

First battalion. The Royal Warwickshire Regiment.
Second batt. The Seaforth Highlanders (Rosshire Buffs, The Duke of Albany's)
First batt. Princess Victoria's (Royal Irish Fusiliers)
Second batt. The Royal Dublin Fusiliers
Tenth Field Ambulance - RAMC

The different companies of our own battalion were allocated individual barns. "C" company halted at the barn I had been sent to, so from this point on "C" company was to be my home. Going amongst them, I found that they were a really fine group of lads and they put me at ease in quite a short time.

Now, being time for sleep, I began to prepare for bed on a great pile of hay. My valise, propped up by my boots, made a substitute pillow. An oil-sheet opened out, formed a rough makeshift sheet, whilst my overcoat on top provided a poor impersonation of a blanket, but better than nothing.

After half an hour I had more than this discomfort to worry about. I began to itch all over and sleep was impossible. Only the next morning did I appreciate the reasons for the irritations of the night, when I saw all the old soldiers stripping off their shirts to hunt out the lice. I copied their example and found plenty. Lice were in my shirt, vest, pants, socks and trousers.

For the first time in my life, I was as lousy as a rook, smothered from head to foot in body lice, having never before even seen one. I felt sick at the mere thought of these vile little creatures crawling all over me. Every time my skin touched clothing, the thought was there and I shivered. My arms would involuntarily move, shoulders rotate, chest would be shifted, legs shaken and feet stamped. Even when nothing was present my imagination would take over and the sensation was real. My God, "If one night in an old barn could produce this, what would happen in the future?" I decided not to worry about the future, but to try and keep myself as clean as possible by frequent bodily inspections at every available opportunity.

It was now time for we 'draft' men to fall in for the morning inspection by the colonel. When we were finally lined up, he made his appearance and stood silently gazing at us all, as sheep ready for the slaughter. Little did I know then, the accuracy of that thought!

He set about the usual top-ranking lecture by reminding us, "You are now with a fighting battalion, which has fought in all corners of the world, has won more battle honours than can be counted, and it is now up to you to uphold this glorious reputation, and uphold the great traditions of your regiment, by doing your duty as soldiers." A little reminder was then added, "For any act of cowardice, you will be shot without hesitation, so if your fate is to die, let it be in battle: carry on sergeant major."

As he quickly walked away, it crossed my mind, "Thanks for that confidential little chat of encouragement, after all, I have offered my services and assistance with our nation's problems, you could have said thank-you!" — God, I had a lot to learn!

Tune of auld lang syne

We're here because, we're here because,
we're here because we're here,
We're here because, we're here because,
we're here because we're here,

Six

Mons - Belgium - *Front Line*

22 OCTOBER 1914

We spent most of the time in billets getting to know each other and chatting about what we thought might happen. The hours passed quickly and soon it was time to leave for our first tour of duty in the trenches. As part of the First Battalion, R.War.R we were now to relieve the Dublin Fusiliers. After receiving our rations of tea, sugar, raw bacon, a one pound loaf of bread, bully beef, cheese, tin of jam, etc. we were ready to go.

At approximately eight o'clock pm on Thursday 22 October, we started our journey. Most of the war was above ground and it was necessary to get as close to the front as we could, before finding any form of created cover, or the protection of a 'support' trench. The old soldiers were full of fun and good cheer, I couldn't share it however and remained quiet and subdued. They knew what to expect, I didn't. As our march progressed, we drew closer and closer to the front line, somewhere south of Mons.

Star shells were being fired into the air and occasional rifle fire could be heard. At a point where we finally approached the support trenches, was a cross roads, congested with troops, some coming from the main trench system, some going to it.

The Germans were adopting the practice of firing a burst from a machine gun at this roadway intersection, with time intervals of about ten minutes, they hoped to catch a few of our troops off guard. Invariably, they were very successful, for each night we had a considerable number killed or wounded.

It must be remembered, that full communication trenches had not yet been dug this early in the war. At the present time we had only a partial cover, in what were mostly shallow affairs and not always continuous. It was necessary to leave one trench, walk over the top and get into the next, walk to the end of that one and out again for another.

Only the smaller men were fully covered by the sides of the trench. Heads therefore were mostly unprotected for taller men. By raking this busy sector at intervals, with a few hundred fast fired rounds at ground level, it was difficult for the German guns to miss.

As I reached this infamous spot, a stream of machine gun bullets came hissing by, at what for me, was head height. Instinctively I stooped to duck my head below the communication trench wall. Unfortunately, a huge Irishman saw me do it.

"Sure and be Jasus, stand up to it like a man," he called, in humiliating tone. So I stood up and learned the mortifying feeling of staring death in the eye. Three of our men were killed and several wounded, but the fearless idiot of an Irishman still stood upright, with a broad grin on his face.

We moved on up a sunken road and out into the open, because we had run out of trenches, then quietly made our way over a field of growing mangel wurzels, which we slipped on and tripped over in the darkness.

Our journey to relieve the Dublin Fusiliers, or the "Dubs" as they came to be known, was continued, but, before we had reached their trench, the Dubs opened up a final rapid fire on the German trench, as it seems, was their customary practice upon being relieved. This caused the Germans to retaliate with a savagely heavy fire, whilst we were pressing on with our effort to reach and relieve the entrenched Dubs, and whilst we were still in the open on top of the trench system.

The Warwick's took the full force of this enemy retaliation and we suffered casualties of thirty men, injured or killed. Why so many wives became widows, or children became fatherless, for such mindless, thoughtless, idiotic behaviour, I never could reason. The Dubs had this crazy notion that they should send a goodnight 'wake-up' signal to the German trench, to mark their pending departure.

No doubt more notices would have gone out to distraught families regretting that their loved ones had been killed in action! Were there no officers aware of this practice? Should we have continued being at risk of death, by the loony hand of our own side, as well as the enemy?

When I finally entered the front line, I had a feeling that my hair was standing on end and I was more than thankful to be under cover. This trench was substantial and deep. Our company was placed out in various bays at intervals of approximately five hundred yards, and sentries were posted. As I was next for duty, it seemed like a good opportunity to have a look around until called. It was too dark however, to distinguish much detail, so I returned to my own post.

The first sentries had finished their two hours duty and I was now 'On.' I was at last an official sentry guarding a section of my trench. Well, this was it. I stood on the 'firing step,' an elevated step-section of the trench wall that gave a standing-height position. It gave full vision for viewing and shooting the enemy over the sandbagged parapet. Thus began my first tour of duty in the firing line.

I looked out across No-Man's-Land, but could see only our own barbed wire. Standing there, in what seemed to be a most unnatural silence, it was hard to stop my mind drifting back to thoughts of home. Liz, mother, father, brothers and sisters.

What would they be doing now? My brothers in the army of course could also be in a battle area somewhere. I had no idea where that might be, as for the rest, since it was now past midnight, they would all be tucked away in their comfortable beds, no doubt fast asleep. What sort of a bloody fool would curse the sergeant major for not sending him out here earlier; enough of that Harry! What the hell did I know! I hadn't been in action or under bombardment and I hadn't seen anything yet. I had asked for it and now I had got it, so, make the best of it mate!

Still looking out across No-Man's-Land I raised my rifle, took careful aim at a large rat and gently squeezed the trigger. This little diversion made me feel better, I had now fired my first round from a front line and we were one rat less. An earlier additional 'first' had been collecting wood and water with which to cook our rations over the charcoal fire in the trench. I muttered softly to myself, "I am here on guard duty 1554 Fred, and I have just shot my first rat, what useful action are you up to?"

Next relief, up went the new sentry, time for me to climb down and crawl into a small narrow dugout and try to get the permitted four hours sleep. It was not possible however, my feet felt like two blocks of ice and the rats scampered about everywhere, even over me. These Belgian rats have no respect. I wonder if I woke all these up when I shot their mate?

I was still awake four hours later, then once more mounting the firing step, with more time to think and nothing to see. It was however, beginning to get a little lighter as dawn started to break and I could see an orange coloured streak across the sky. Such a surprisingly pretty effect of light, triggered a happy memory from my sixth, or was it my seventh, birthday. I must have been seven because the year was 1902.

Presents were a rarity at that time, money was too short with a large family to keep, but that day I had a present from my Mum. She had made it herself. Usually, any presents we received, or gave, consisted of something we were passing on, either because it no longer fitted, or had ceased to be appropriate. By this means everything went down to the next smallest child, to avoid waste. This was different. This was a present just for me, for my birthday.

As the family gathered around, I took my present from the paper bag into which it had been carefully folded and held it up for all to see. It was a new waistcoat. "Try it on, Harry"! Mum said and quite excitedly I let my sixteen year old sister Polly, feed my arms into the spaces and she buttoned me up. I loved it; colourful; horizontally striped in orange and black.

It was my elder brother Jack, who broke the silence, when he roared with laughter, the tears streaming down his cheeks as he looked at me posed in my display.

"What's the matter Jack? Don't you like it?" Mum questioned.

"Yes!" He spluttered, "But it's our Harry, with those stripes, he looks just like a little Perch." He then convulsed into more laughter.

Frank, only two years younger than Jack, looked up

"He does; he does" he agreed and also folded into laughter as soon as the image registered.

"I always thought there was something fishy about him!" said Jack as he wiped his eyes.

"Stop teasing him, you two" Polly demanded, but it was all too much for me. I flew at Jack with little arms flailing like a windmill, in a full frontal attack. Jack, then an 'old man' of 23, wrapped his arms around me and held me close to his chest as he spun around and around, with me unable to move or escape. I screwed up my nose and gave him a fierce look saying

"I'll get you our Jack" which in my totally helpless state, set everyone into fits of laughter.

"The little Perch, thinks he's a big fierce Pike," said Jack wiping another tear on his shirt sleeve "But it's a lovely waistcoat Mum," then he added "I really love it Harry." Without releasing me, he squeezed me tightly to him saying "And I love you too, little Perch!"

"I'm still going to get you, our Jack" was all I could say and everyone dissolved once more into happy laughter.

The moist cloud was now in my eyes, as the orange glow in the sky became diluted by the developing ground mist. Perch I then was, and for a long time after that, Perch I remained. I smiled to myself and muttered "Thanks Jack, and you Frank, God bless you both!"

The greyness was getting much lighter. I could now make out the German wire, and then the German trench. I wondered; were they over there looking at me? Another first, this was my first glimpse of the enemy, or at least, where they were. Little did I know then, that I would still be looking at them, three and a half years later.

Dawn and the whole battalion stood-to in the event of an attack. The Germans had sent us rapid fire and we retaliated. Some of our number went down after being hit, we don't know how many. Perhaps we hit some of the Germans, who knows! The only certainty is that our wounded will have to stay where they are for a few hours. They can never be taken out of the trenches for medical treatment until night time, it would be absolute madness to negotiate the wurzel field in daylight.

Later on, it appeared that the anticipated attack would not take place after all. Strange! A rapid fire was almost always followed by an attack. Incidentally, I was later told, that during our wait for darkness on this occasion, three of our wounded lads had died.

Six days after this we were relieved by another company. We did not however, follow the bad example set by the Dubs in sending a goodnight greeting to the Germans. Comrades were not therefore exposed to return fire during their arrival. Our exit was as quiet as we could make it and they all got in without casualty. The objective was now the mangel wurzel field, the cross roads and the shallow trenches, for six days to be spent in support.

I suffered an accidental smack in the eye from a 'slung' rifle during our journey in darkness and my feet were getting worse, particularly my right foot. One of the old soldiers looked at it and said

"Well, what I think is, you've got a bit of frostbite in there." The pain became unbearable, so the first night in support, I got into my dugout, took off my right boot and wrapped a blanket around my foot to keep it warm.

After a short time CSM Jeffries poked his head around the edge of my dugout to warn me that I was on the next ration party. He caught sight of my boot in the corner and with a note of absolute horror he gasped!

"You've-got-your-boot-off! You will see the captain when we get back to billets," I smiled, when he had gone. It didn't seem to me a particularly serious matter.

Ration fatigue now over, I snatched a few hours sleep before stand-to at dawn. We had quite an easy time of it during the day, but we had to keep under cover. Six days in support, then we moved back further from the front, for six days in reserve. Nothing interesting ever happened here and we were glad to pack our bags and march to our billets. It was back to the good old barn at La Crêche with its miniature livestock, after eighteen days at the front.

On the second day in billets I received a severe shock. Up came the sergeant major screaming

"YOU! Company Orders." I arrived there to hear the CSM give his evidence. **"SIR**, I went to warn 1553 Private Morgan for ration party and found him in his dugout with his **BOOT OFF."**

The captain gave me a strange look of incredulity. I felt like a criminal.

"Anything to say?" He asked,

"Only to say sir, that my foot was frozen and I wrapped a blanket around it to try and warm it a little."

"You should not have done that," he said with a shake of his head, "The CSM was under the impression that I could try this case, however, it is far too serious and you will have to see the CO, I'm sorry, I am not permitted to try you myself."

At once, I was escorted to the colonel's office.

"Cap off, quick march, halt." The CSM repeated his evidence and now it was the COs turn to have a go at me.

"I suppose," he said with a distinct note of sarcasm, "Had the enemy attacked, you would have been in your dugout with your boot off!"

"I should have" I started, but had no time to finish the sentence,

"You would have" he snarled,"Fourteen days number two field punishment."

From his office, I was taken to a small brick compartment called the cells. Any hard or particularly dirty work about the area, now had to come my way. I did not expect to be arrested for having frostbite, or whatever it was. Medical treatment would have been welcome.

Had the malady worsened, I would have been unable to move at all, and perhaps lost a leg, what good would that have been to the war effort. Later on in the war, this malady was to be better known to the troops at the front as "Trench Foot," it was caused mainly from wallowing about in trench water and having continuously wet feet.

They made it quite clear, that *prisoners* like me in the front line, were given all the jobs that might have resulted in death, as part of their penance. Not a pleasant thought, particularly as I would still be classed as a prisoner when soon we returned to the front line. I could then be on outposts, advanced lookouts, patrols, barbed-wiring and many more delightful excursions.

Our six days billeting period soon ended, and we moved forward again to the front line. This time we managed to make it with only two casualties, both wounded whilst crossing from one trench to another. We had just arrived and barely settled down when Captain Wasey came up the trench, calling for the prisoners, he selected five, including me and Dickey Poole. This was a chap I got on with very well and we seemed to have a similar sense of humour, not fully appreciated by everyone.

Captain Wasey on the other hand, was what might be called, outside the film industry, a chance taker, with an almost total disregard of his own life, or anyone else's, a real life daredevil. There was not much of him, a slim five foot four, but wiry, serious and to put it kindly, more than a little reckless.

"Follow me" he commanded.

None of us were pleased to be there, but given little choice, we trudged along behind him in silence. Our direction was straight along to the end of the trench, over the parapet and across No-Man's-Land, until we were directly behind the German trenches. Like us, they had discontinuous trench systems, the trenches were not in one line, they were in groups with outposts about five hundred yards apart.

Neither did their trenches always connect with each other. Each company held its own trench with a gap between each one, of about two hundred yards. Now of course, we were behind the enemy, crawling in the mud on our stomachs. We had no idea what the captain intended to do, or what he expected us to do. But we soon found out. "Whatever happens," he whispered, "follow me". Creeping nearer to the German trench, he located the centre of his attention, which was a machine gun post.

Drawing two bombs from his belt, he set the pointers to fire and threw one on the gun, but the other fell short and brought shrapnel hissing its way back to us, thankfully also wide of a target. Leaping to his feet he ran back towards our own lines, with his patrol easily keeping pace with him.

All went well until we reached the half way point in No-Man's-Land. The Germans wasted no time in opening up a rapid fire. Throwing ourselves flat to the rough ground, the bullets whistled over our heads.

This was followed up by a salvo of shrapnel shells, which exploded in the air and being designed to shatter, forcefully showered the deadly, jagged, metal fragments downwards over a wide spread. Two members of our patrol were hit and wounded. Eventually, we were able to carry them back to our own trench when things quietened down.

I'd had enough of Captain Wasey for the time being, I never could stand this Douglas Fairbanks attitude, so I crept back into my dugout. There was to be no rest however, for a 'one boot' criminal! I was immediately warned for 'ration party,' after which I was granted two hours sleep before once more mounting the firing step for sentry duty.

At least I had plenty of time to think, out on the 'step,' and could always get in a bit more practice with the rats. What a pity I could not haul them all in afterwards and line them up on the parapet. We could keep a record, or even have a competition! I yawned, stretched, and told myself to just keep looking for movements, and the enemy.

Are we down hearted? ———no
So let your voices ring- and all together sing
Are we downhearted ?- no
Not while Britannia rules the waves - Not likely
While we've Jack upon the sea
and Tommy on the on the land we'll be impressed,
It's a long long way to Tipperary,
but we are not downhearted yet.

Seven

My Nineteenth Birthday

21 November 1914

The firing step was always a good place for thinking. There's something about the solitude and quietness of the landscape. Just standing, letting my eyes follow the uneven contours of the ground, seeing the miles of barbed wire twisting and turning its way across the undulations, it seems sufficient to induce the question "Is anybody out there?"

We seldom saw anyone, yet there must have been thousands of troops, our own and those of the enemy. All living and moving below ground, off the skyline, out of sight. Viewing life and each other through periscopes. I felt like a mole.

Before getting too carried away, it dawned upon me that tomorrow was Saturday, the twenty first of November 1914. My birthday, and I would be nineteen years old. What a way to spend a birthday.

I glanced down at my boot, what a pity, if only they would grant me just one birthday wish, I would request that this, now muddy, (but beautifully blackened underneath) boot, could be given the "freedom of the trench," to find the most tender spot on the rear of the CO, who granted my fourteen days punishment! What the hell! There was no use fretting. It had to be accepted. "Just look at those bloody rats out there!"

My two hours completed I handed over my duty to the next man 'On' and reported to the CSM. I might have guessed that we criminals could not get off as lightly as other mortals he needed me for a wiring party. Over the top and out we went. Having crawled around with our new rolls of wire, we patched and closed any gaps we found.

This took about two hours and lasted as long as the remaining hours of darkness. Now of course we had a great deal more wire out in front of us to help slow down intruders and stem enemy attacks. I had never seen so much barbed wire, what a waste of time, of effort and of materials. The thought occurred that whoever manufactured this was pleased to have a war! It was by then early daylight and stand-to. What a good job criminals don't need to sleep!

The Germans were not too happy about our raid on their machine gun post and gave us a busy ten minutes answering their rapid fire. They were certainly crack shots, their bullets constantly ripping the top off our sandbags. When a casual bullet hit the sand bag just in front of my face, I decided to accept that discretion was the better part of valour and left the firing step for the trench. The gunfire gradually decreased and died away, almost as if they had tired of the chore and found something better to do.

A German soldier from their trench suddenly gave out with a realistic impersonation of a crowing cockerel, which amused us all. He also shouted something to us in German. In fact we were to hear from this man each morning at dawn from now on. Perhaps a farm boy feeling homesick? A few of the Warwick's answered back with something in our language, but most certainly from the 'Troops' Concise, not the 'Oxford.'

Daylight at last and peace for everyone, even prisoners. The sergeant major was reluctant to move about in the daytime, so we could enjoy the same periods of rest as all the others. The letter delivery had been brought up with the rations overnight and I received a card from my mother. It was meant to cheer me up and probably would have, arriving as it did on my birthday. However, being still the 'one boot' prisoner, I felt down at heart.

I read that card over and over again, until I knew it from memory. I know it was a commercial one that she had adapted to her own sentiments, but I also knew her well enough to be aware that she meant every single word. It went:

"Dear Boy,
When evening shadows fall and working hours go by,
I long to hear your step again and wish that you were nigh,
But you have answered duties call and pride holds back my tears,
I live in hope of your return, and peaceful, happy, years."

Words I shall never forget. God Bless her. With six sons fighting in this war, every woman would understand the torture she must have been going through, expecting to hear at any time, that one or other of us had gone under. Younger brother Fred was now settled into the cavalry, the last of us to join the army, but I have no idea at all where any of them are, or how they are!

The next week or two was also a quiet period of time, which gave us a breathing space in which to carry out repairs and trench improvements. Generally, not a lot was happening at present, except for a German raid on our trench, not a serious one, perhaps they had nothing to do either. It was just a nuisance raid in fact and easily stopped: What a good job we had laid all that incredibly useful barbed wire out there!

If you want the Sergeant Major, I know where he is,
I know where he is, I know where he is
If you want the Sergeant Major, I know where he is,
He's hanging on the old barbed wire
I've seen him, I've seen him, hanging on the old barbed wire,
I've seen him, I've seen him, hanging on the old barbed wire,

Eight

Surprise Celebration

Christmas Eve 1914

It was Christmas Eve, 24 December 1914, when we returned to the front line. We did not expect miracles and yet an incredible thing was about to happen, for which we were totally unprepared.

During stand-to, at the hour of dawn on Christmas Day, one thing was particularly noticeable. There was no rapid fire, in fact no firing at all, only an unreal silence. We were all aware of it and those not on duty came out from their dugouts to see why it was so quiet. No guns! No bullets! No voices: Nothing. The spell was broken by the now customary cockcrow from the German trench, but then another German soldier shouted out from his section "Come over here Warwick's!" in absolutely perfect English. One of our lads called back "How's your Father - Fritz?" to be met with the response, "Then meet me half way."

Looking over the parapet, we could see that he had left his trench and was standing on the top bank, in the open and in full view. He then walked towards us and stood in the middle of No-Man's-Land. He either had full confidence in the Christian spirit of Christmas Day, or was completely round the twist but, whatever it was, we admired his guts. One of our company followed suit and went out to meet him and there they were, shaking hands like a couple of long lost school chums.

It was unbelievable. In no time at all, a whole crowd of Germans had left their trench and gathered around the two of them, where eventually, the whole of my company assembled. To cap it all Jack Reagan, a civilian barber, had taken a chair with him and was giving haircuts mid barbed wire in No-Man's-Land which was suddenly full of troops from both sides, exchanging cigarettes for bully beef.

The German soldier I was with gave me his cigarette case, in exchange for a tin. He thought that was a great prize. Officers came out as well, from both sides, the English officers used the pretext of getting the men back again, or going out to meet them half way to prevent the enemy seeing our trench system, but they were also shaking hands with the German officers, who no doubt used the same excuse for their own presence.

Some men went back to their trench and returned with spades to give a decent burial to the dead. It had been too dangerous previously to make the attempt in daylight and now both sides were here, working together. The Germans made much more of Christmas than we did. They even made some considerable effort to decorate the top of their trench with paper lanterns, and sung seasonal songs, which were pleasant to listen to. They called to us to respond, which some sections of the trench did. It was all most enjoyable and totally unbelievable.

Finally it was all ended and we had to get back. It was a little later in the day that our officer came through the trench to present us all with an unexpected gift from home. It was from HRH The Princess Mary and I thought at the time that it was presented to all members of the British Expeditionary Force. An embossed brass box containing a pipe, twenty cigarettes, one ounce of tobacco, a tinder lighter, Christmas card and a photograph of the young lady responsible for such a lovely thought, bless her heart.

I had never smoked a pipe before, but made a start on that one to celebrate the occasion. The box was strongly made and I vowed to look after it, the best way I could, and take it home whenever the opportunity came, to show my parents. It was a lovely surprise and much appreciated.[1]

For the next two or three weeks not a shot was fired within half a mile of us. It was as if we had decided to end the fighting all by ourselves. Could it really have happened like this? If all the troops along the line had refused to fight, on both sides, would the war have ended there and then? With officers on each side in support, if we had all walked away at that point, could the result have been a truce? I doubt it, but it's a thought.

We could see the Germans boldly walking about on the top of their trench still, but we wouldn't fire at them. Some of us ventured to copy their trench-top walking, and the Germans also held firm to our joint new found trust in each other. However, this pleasurable affair eventually came to an abrupt end.

A German soldier was walking along his parapet carrying a bucket when one of the members of my company further up the line, took deliberate aim and shot him. Inevitable perhaps, ordered maybe, but I felt unhappy that it was one of us that had broken the unwritten trust. The unfortunate man had no sooner hit the ground, when they hit us with everything they had, a rapid fire to exceed all previous rapid firings.

The war was on again with a vengeance. They yelled at us, calling us "English swine" and many other insults mostly in German but in English if they felt the words were bad or strong enough. In addition, they gave us, and the Dubs absolute hell when we went through the relieving process in the future. I felt strongly aware at that time, that it was indeed a fine line, that divided the processed training of official killers for wartime, from the mindful killing of predetermined murder!

---

[1] see appendix one

I want to go home, I want to go home,
I don't want to go in the trenches no more
where whiz-bangs and shrapnel will whistle and roar
Take me over the sea, where the Allemande can't get at me
Oh my I don't want to die, I want to go home.

Nine

Ploegsteert

January 1915

The fighting made its continuous but uncertain progress during the latter part of January 1915. We were now back in billets, at a place called Ploegsteert, (about four miles NNW of Armentières) though it was always known as 'Plug Street' to the troops. The weather was bitterly cold, so we took a few pieces of wood, including a worm eaten barn door that we found laying around over the floor of the barn we were in, to make a small fire.

The farmer went spare. He then complained to the colonel, and that resulted in a fine of two francs for each of us. The wood was fit for nothing but burning. The place looked a lot tidier after it had gone, and we had stopped the spread of wood worm through the rest of the building. We had really done him a favour.

The money however, was not enough to satisfy the anger of the farmer. He took the handle off the old water pump, so that we were unable to draw any water. In reprisal, an unknown avenger, who shall remain unknown, dropped hundreds of small stones down the barrel of his pump, which meant that neither could he!

Only on two occasions did we go into the front line trenches from Ploegsteert. The first time was standard duty and without event. The second was more specific, when an advance party of the Argyll and Sutherland Highlanders came with us for trench instruction. They were a territorial battalion and still used the less efficient Canadian Ross, long rifle, not the shorter barrelled Lee Enfields that we used. This must have placed them at a great disadvantage in battle.

As I walked up the trench I could see one of their sergeants looking through a sniping plate

"For Gods sake don't look through there sergeant," I warned him, "The Germans can put a bullet right through that sighting hole anytime they feel like it."

Turning his head to look at me, I could tell from his expression that he didn't take too kindly to a private instructing a sergeant, especially one of my age.

"Mon de ye think he could hit such a wee spot from that distance?" Barely were the words out of his mouth, when a bullet came through the hole and smacked into a sandbag on the opposite side of the trench. As he looked unbelievingly at the sandbag, he also noticed the hollowed out concave shape into which, not only that particular bullet had smacked, but also many others.

He was fully aware of his close shave with sudden death. The shot would have hit him between the eyes. He was shattered and found it impossible to believe, until I explained the situation.

"The Germans have a series of rifles firmly fixed on iron tripods. The sights being carefully pre-set and aimed at our various sniping plates, all along the trench. Anyone on duty over there simply has to walk up the row pulling an occasional trigger and there is a high chance that someone in our trench will catch for it. You know sergeant," I said to him, "we have found it to be far safer to fire from over the top parapet of the trench, rather than use the steel plates; at least the guns countering that, are hand held and stand a fair chance of missing their target." He was truly delighted that I had spoken out and put him right in good time.

The remainder of the Argyll's came in and we moved back to our old billets for the last time. The next day after a good clean up, we started our march to Oultersteene, some five kilometres from Bailleul where we had been promised a rest! We received plenty of hard training instead.

There was to be no rest for us that day, only at night, and thanks to the lice which were continually on the attack, we had no rest even then. A chance to clean up and change clothing was always welcome of course, but under these conditions we were again just as lousy within half an hour.

Within about five weeks of continued hard training, we were made up to full fighting strength from the new intake of Warwickshire Territorials who had recently arrived in France. Forming up in the square, we received hearty cheers from the 'new lads' before setting off on our journey. We were now on our way to an attack at Ieper, as the Belgians call it, (with an I not an L) or Ypres, as the French would have it, or as our lads insisted, 'WIPERS,' where the British were presently fighting to the last man. The Germans had been unexpectedly striving to break through, which upset the original Allied plan for a combined Spring offensive this year, in 1915.

This surprise German attack, had hit the Ypres salient on 22 April 1915, just a short time ago. A minimal bombardment from seventeen inch Howitzers, was followed by yellowish-green clouds of poisonous chlorine gas. This was the first time chlorine gas had been used on the Western front.

More than 500 cylinders had been opened and 168 tons of pressurised gas released into the prevailing wind, to drift over Allied trenches, leaving in its trail 5,000 men killed and 10,000 injured.

So far the British position was being successfully held. We now understood that our task was to reinforce this situation and put the enemy on the defensive by way of a tactical change. What that would be, we couldn't guess. No doubt this would now be the responsibility of the new commander of 10th Brigade Major-General C.P.Hull.

Gassed last night and gassed the night before,
Goner get gassed tonight if we never get gassed any more
When we're gassed, we're sick as we can be
Phosgene and Mustard gas is much too much for me
They're warning us, they're warning us, one respirator for the four of us
Thank your lucky stars that three of us, can run,
So one of us can use it all alone

Ten

Second Battle of Ypres — *22 Apl to 25 May*

25 April 1915

It proved to be a long march from Bailleul to the town of Ypres in Belgium, but from the start the battalion looked in fine trim. We reached the outskirts at about one o'clock in the morning on Sunday 25 April 1915 and 'fell-out' on the side of the road. Heavy rain, which we were now getting used to, followed us most of the way.

The sounds of battle could be heard and it was obviously not too far away. Our Artillery were streaming their shells over as fast as they could be loaded, as if trying to close the gaps between each shell. Those gun barrels must have been close to melting point.

Wounded soldiers were constantly walking, limping, or being carried away from the town, past our rest area. Three men in tartan kilts came along together, assisting each other on their painful journey, uniforms ripped and tattered. All of them were covered in mud and blood.

"Who are you fellers with?" One of our lads called as they drew closer. Of the three, a tall man whose left arm hung limply at his side, while his right arm supported a wounded colleague, replied without stopping,

"We're all that's left of a Company of Canadian Scottish! A second gas attack yesterday, finished us!"

"Bloody hell," gasped our lad.

"Yes it is!" said another of the three. "You're right there bud, a very bloody hell."

"We've got some hopes then, we're just on our way in."

The reply to this was simple and sincerely intended:

"God help you in there then mates, keep your gas masks handy."

The enemy had begun to shell the town of Ypres. Buildings were bursting open, flinging masonry and other projectiles over a wide area. Whole structures were crumbling and caving in. Flames leapt from the beautiful, massive structure of St.Maartens Cathedral and the even larger old Cloth Hall. Half of the town was on fire; a vast inferno, whilst the other half appeared to have charred and crumbled like match-wood into great heaps of rubble.

My feelings were contradictory, on the one hand I felt desperately sorry for the townsfolk, men women and children who might have been in there. Yet, no doubt due to my lack of worldly experience, I sat on the roadside absolutely spellbound. I felt it was the most awe inspiring, wonderful vision I had ever seen in my life.

I was fascinated by the sight of such large scale destruction, and at the same time ashamed of my immediate reaction, to the sheer obscenity of it. However, even a thoughtless youth could not avoid being moved by the scene that followed. Along the road and now passing us, were the townsfolk from Ypres. Old men and women pushing handcarts, filled with whatever could be saved from their homes. From another direction through the fields, came others carrying huge bundles of clothing, all that they now possessed. Poor old ladies, just like my mother, carrying grandchildren, as well as whatever they had managed to salvage. Their hearts broken, loved ones lost, in the bombardment of their beloved town. Hundreds of people had now been killed or buried alive.

Families had been eliminated, gone, along with everything they had worked hard for during their lives. I looked at these faces, wet with the tears still being shed, now diluted by the falling rain. Bodies soaked, feet and legs covered in mud. Some were lucky enough to have shoes or clogs on their feet, others went without. I was thankful when the last one had gone by. They brought my inner feelings of disgust to a head.

Crabby Freeman, an older more experienced veteran sitting near, saw my face. Aware of my reaction to it all, he said

"Don't let it affect you Harry, we all tend to think to ourselves that it could be our own kin, but be thankful it ain't. We've got our job to do so we can make sure it ain't. None of us knows who will get it next, it might be the local people, it might be us, we are all taking the same chance mate, and we are after the people what did it." I knew what he was saying and tried to believe it. I nodded and he walked away. A simple question formed in my mind, "Why should this be happening to anyone?" What had these poor people done to deserve it?

Ypres. - The Cloth Halls, with the Cathedral in the background, as they were before the First World War.

Ypres. - The same viewpoint at the end of the war.

My platoon officer, 2nd Lt. Danson who appeared to be no older than me, came along to gather his men together and to give us final instructions for the attack.

"Well, you fellows" he began, "I want now to give you an idea of what we have to do at dawn! The Brigade is concentrated upon the retaking of St Julien and the 1st Warwick's are left of the line, with the 7th Argyll and Sutherland's in support. Our "C" Company has its own position to attack, and it simply has GOT to be taken. That is our direct responsibility. The main attack on St. Julien will be carried out by the Seaforths, Irish Fusiliers and Dublin Fusiliers, to our right.

Ours is a strategically important woodland area, six hundred yards wide and one hundred yards long. There is a village at the far end of the wood, which we also HAVE to take then dig ourselves in at the front of the village. So there it is, that is all we have to do, then we will be relieved by another Regiment. Any questions?"

Tubby Ingram, another veteran grumbled,

"We've had some wood fighting before sir, in this sector there won't be anyone left for them to relieve!"

"All right," Lt. Danson replied quietly, "Don't give me a bad time chaps, this is my first battle and like most of you, my mother has instructed me to get back home safely, we will all do our best I am sure."

It was still raining and we were all soaked through to the skin when every man was given a double issue of rum. It was strong stuff, and now we felt ready for the whole German army. We fell in and moved off towards Ypres, past the old Cloth Hall, which may once have been the old centre of the town's woollen industry, but it would not see those days again.

It was burning and crumbling, fierce flames illuminated the night sky and everything else within sight, including us. As timber structures collapsed and fell into the white hot inferno, great clouds of sparks rose up on the thermals created by the heat, like a monstrous firework display. Behind it, little could be seen of the Cathedral except even more flames. We could feel the heat. It was an outrageous and unbelievable sight!

On we continued across fields, from which the heavy rains could not drain. The water simply soaked into the thin crust of top soil to penetrate and mix with the clay beneath. The result was a deep sticky mud that was everywhere. These same fields were later to become vast graveyards. Still, we went forward towards St.Julien.

At the present time this whole area was simply littered with the rotting corpses of the dead. Some were propped up by their valises. Others were spread-eagled and face down, many were doubled up, features contorted, having died in considerable agony. There seemed to be hundreds of them.

Truly a horrifying sight to behold. No glory or honour about this and certainly no dignity. Just twisted, mangled, disfigured remnants of human flesh, bone and blood. Many of them were the Canadians we had earlier been told about, whose misfortune it had been, to face the first German gas attack; so, this was the result!

The words of Crabby to Lt. Danson had new meaning. I felt after seeing this, that I would never leave Ypres alive. Any one of those bodies could be me. I was pleased to have my attention drawn by the battalion who were now spreading out. "A" company marched off to the left, "B" company half left, "C" company half right and "D" company marched to the right.

It was obvious that we were somewhere near the action. It must now have been about 4-30am. A white 'Verey' light was shot from a pistol some three hundred yards to our left, tracing its own trajectory into the black sky before bursting into a brilliant star. We were suddenly in artificial daylight. "What sort of a bloody fool did that," I muttered, then realised that we were now actually in action. The Germans had fired the light as a signal to their troops to open fire on us; and my God, what a fire it was! In three seconds all hell was let loose.

Their Artillery gave us the full power of their shells in a continuous salvo of 'drum fire' that seemed to go on forever. Machine guns kept up a rapid fire, sweeping and strafing at ground level, as if they never needed a belt change. We were in a deadly crossfire and the air was alive with the sinister hiss of active bullets.

The German 'whiz-bang' 77s gave the usual preliminary warning we could recognise. Normally we would have had a few seconds to dive for cover as these shells arrived, but they were not alone. The 77s were lightweight field pieces, usually firing shrapnel shells, but that sound was now lost, within the cocktail of all the available German firing power comprising the 'drum-fire.'

There were 'crumps,' as we called them from the Howitzers, massive guns with huge fat shells that seemed to go straight into the air, then drop down again. The trajectory of these being so severe and the speed so slow, that it was possible in daylight to see the shells in flight.

Neither could we distinguish these shells from the 5.9s we called coalboxes,' which also gave a little time for shelter, just before the deep roar at the end of their journey indicated a rapid descent back to earth. Everything the Germans had was now directed at us and we could do nothing!

Three quarters of my company fell. Kicking, struggling, moaning, cursing, writhing and screaming with pain. The four in front of me all went down together, falling across each other almost without a sound. I could not believe that it was real. Dumbfounded, I just stood there, until a bullet struck the front of my steel helmet and made it spin halfway round my head. In panic I leapt for cover behind the four who fell.

Recovering from my fear, I moved closer to the heap of bodies. I could hear and feel, the shallow thump, thump, thump, of yet more bullets slamming into these already dead men. It was not possible for me to get any closer, so pressing myself to the muddy ground and trying to melt into it, was my only alternative.

Others in the company had leaped into water filled shell holes, or similarly, were sheltering behind the dead. Many in fact would find it impossible to get back out of the shell holes, and would eventually slide further and further down the mud walls, only to drown at the bottom in the soft glutinous depths at the core.

If only I could get back to that shallow ditch I had seen a few yards away, I felt I would be much safer. Looking at it and at the two strands of barbed wire in front, it looked formidable, but seemed to be my only chance. Now I had to use my head.

The machine guns were enfilading, so I needed to wait for the one dangerous to me, to fire over my head. From that time, I would have until the arc was completed, to the point of reverse. The swing would then return to my present position and go past in the opposite direction. I needed to know the length of time that this movement took.

Awaiting the hissing bullets to fly right over my head, I counted in rough seconds the delay before the bullets returned to me. Now I knew how long I had, in order to make that dash for the ditch, about nine seconds: Not a long time! The bullets returned, I jumped to my feet as soon as they went over my head, all the time counting out loud as I ran, holding my rifle in front of my body to hurl myself at the wire. The top strand of wire broke and I fell head first into the ditch with just three seconds left to count, before bullets ripped through the grass bank above my head once more.

Providing I could avoid being hit by a shell, I was at least safe for the time being. My trousers were torn and my legs were bleeding from the wire barbs. I knew that earlier this month the Lewis machine gun MK1 had been introduced, and distribution would follow. If only I had been given one of those at this time, I could certainly have evened the score, and fought back.

Within a short time, I was surprised and quite pleased to see that some others from the battalion were joining me, in my little ditch. They had been given the "official" order to retire, by their officer, who was now also joining us. Apparently, he still felt unsafe. So unsafe, that he gave an additional order to retire further back. In trouble I might be, but daft I was not, it didn't strike me as being a particularly good idea. This was no time to argue however, particularly as I would have lost. I decided to disobey the order, stay where I was, and suffer the consequences later.

The officer, followed by all the men (except one), jumped to the top of the ditch and ran. I raised my head sufficiently to see them go to their new retirement position. Sadly, that position for a great many of them, transpired to be prone to the ground for eternity. The machine guns opened up and men were mown down like meadow grass. Hundreds died. That order should never have been given.

In less than ten minutes, the same man gave the order for them all to advance again and low and behold, the remainder once more piled into my little haven. How many were killed in this return trip? I couldn't guess. Two lunatic orders from an inexperienced officer, who was struck by extreme panic.

I was now full of relief and self congratulation for staying in my muddy shelter, for which I was gaining a close affection, but not for long. The order came down the line to "ADVANCE." Unavoidably, I leaped out with all the others and we moved forward in two long lines. An unbelievable reception awaited us, which was indescribable. Except to say it was simply hell.

With our own platoon officer 2nd Lt. Danson in the front, leading the first line, I was directly behind, but fortunately in the second line and therefore avoided the explosion of the shell that fell upon him and the men near to him. We all dived to the ground to avoid shrapnel, then rose up to continue the advance.

I passed close to what remained of Lt. Danson, now just a torso, with the men near him unidentifiably scattered over a considerable distance. Someone would have to write and tell the lieutenant's mum why he could not obey her instruction!

We were making for a German trench and carried on moving towards it. A replacement officer was quickly sent forward to take over from Lt. Danson. "Carry on men! Don't stop! Keep going! We're getting close!" Shells, bullets, shrapnel, all were bursting, hissing and exploding around us, as we continued forward. We were now only ten yards from the German trench when it was my turn to fall. My leg suddenly went in another direction and I fell over, like a one legged man having his crutch kicked away.

I had received a bullet. The pain was considerable and blood was pouring from it. In my prone position, I knew there would be no assistance under these circumstances and tried to stem the blood as much as I could. The lines carried on moving, with many men dropping, never to move again, or wounded, trying to patch themselves up. We were all now quite alone. The columns had moved on, without us.

Now I knew what being shot felt like and it was an experience I could have done without. Another feeling of guilt crept over me. Should I, could I, get to my feet and carry on? There was no way I could have added to our effort and I never was a hero, so I decided to stay where I was, by the German wire. They would have shot me again if I moved anyway.

The battle raged on in front of me. A Scottish soldier with kilt flying out behind him, raced for and entered a small brick building that housed a machine gun. This had been holding up our advance and inflicting a terrific number of casualties, I watched intently as the explosion of a grenade inside the building silenced the gun team. The Scot never reappeared.

One of our officers suddenly launched himself at the enemy from his position forward on my right, shouting at the top of his voice, "Follow me lads" as he leapt into the German trench. He was unlucky, there were none of his lads left - I saw his dead body heaved like a bale of hay, back out of the trench by the German occupants. It looked much as if only a few of the 'lads' I had been with a short time ago, would return to their own lines. The Germans still held the trench.

Dead and dying were sprawled in heaps, all over the fields. When, after some two hours or more, German machine guns prevented our support getting through, our troops were forced to fall back to a line of trenches and consolidate. I lay there helplessly and watched them go back, throw themselves on the ground and use their entrenchment spades. The soil began to rise all along the line, as they cut their way into the soil, to provide more cover.

I had seen death before I came out here, when an uncle died and I saw his body before the burial; that was a respectful, caring matter with a high degree of dignity. I could never in my wildest dreams, have visualised such carnage as this present saturation of wholesale slaughter and annihilation. Or the shock vision of the Canadians we met on the way in. How can the full horror of that be described? But it was shortly to be revealed that I still had seen nothing yet!

The Irish battalion a little further along the Line, was retiring and as I looked on, I saw the German troops leaping out of their trench to charge the retiring Irishmen, thinking them to be completely on the run. However, far from being on the run, the Irish, having led them a good distance out into the field, suddenly stopped, there was a loud command of; – "FIX BAYONETS" before they turned quickly around to face the enemy, who were obviously taken completely by surprise.

Within what seemed only minutes, every German who left the trench and most of the Irishmen, were dead. I was sickened, spiritually and physically, by the sight of bayonets piercing body after body, the noise, the screams, the shouts. I wondered what my own fate would be now, if I was found by the Germans. This would happen if we retired far enough back, and the enemy came out to collect their wounded, or resorted to the usual looting for souvenirs, as happened on both sides.

The time was now about 7-00am and what was left of the British force had dug in deep enough to be protected. They then decided to open up a rapid fire at the Germans, who in turn retaliated with their own rapid fire. I was now right in the middle. It was a total nightmare and for the next hour, I wished myself dead, in order to get the inevitable over with as quickly as possible.

Bullets were swishing through the grass all around me. Some smacked into the barbed wire stumps. I could hear some of the German soldiers laughing, shouting out and joking. Laying flat on my back looking into the sky, I thanked God quietly, when finally the British put their rifles down. They had done no good whatsoever and did more harm to their own wounded out here, than to the well entrenched Germans.

All was now silent. I had a mental image of our lads getting out the bully beef and biscuits. God, how I envied them. I couldn't make a move to get my emergency rations from my haversack. I knew full well that the German sentries would be looking for even the slightest of movements, at which they would shoot without question. I had already seen a few men rise to their feet wounded, delirious, or in shock. They had stumbled about, not knowing which way to go, some groaning and in much pain. A sudden rifle crack from the German line and for them, the war was over.

The rain had started falling again some two hours ago, but it had now got into its swing and was relentless. I didn't know how my wound was doing. My leg was going numb, my body aching all over from the forced attempt to remain still. Soaked to the skin, trembling with fear and cold, the hours slowly ticking by, I fully expected to be shot through the head any second.

There was yet another movement in the field and a moan from one of the more seriously wounded followed by a faint cry for help, though he still lay on the muddy ground. This followed the same pattern as before, a rifle fired and then silence, and this was repeated every time a movement or sound was made. Prisoners were not being taken. I was helplessly trapped.

That day was the longest day of my life. I could not understand why our attack had taken place without artillery support of our own, it seemed most unusual and perhaps this would prove to have been another costly mistake. All my limbs had gone stiff and I was now stuck in the unrelenting mud. Fourteen hours without any movement and the expectancy of being finished off, as callously as those poor unfortunates I had at intervals seen or heard dispatched.

This experience would forever remain deep in my memory. I thought that perhaps when 1554 Fred and I met to compare notes, this could well be the major story of my life. Whatever he might be going through, I was hoping that he would not have to face anything like this. I wouldn't have wished this on my worst enemy. Not even the old sod that punished me for only having one boot on. Well! - Maybe just him. At the same time, I had grave doubts about ever meeting up with Fred, or anyone else for that matter. My chances now of survival were pretty slim!

My rambling mind was next invaded by a reminder that the Germans would come out soon to collect their wounded, if they hadn't shot them all in error. It was now dusk and I tried to turn my head in the direction of the enemy trench which was insufferably close, but my head would not move, my whole body was stuck in the cold, clay-mud and every joint was welded. Panic set in.

Getting desperate now, I tried rocking myself from side to side, to generate some sort of movement without creating a visual image on the skyline. I was already held fast in the mud, which produced a sucking sound when I moved, but the rocking was slowly, but slowly, loosening the muddy grip. For Christ sake don't make a noise, I told myself.

At last I was able to roll over on to my side and then to my stomach, with gritted teeth and barely avoiding the necessity to scream out with the pain from my wound and every other part of my cramped, confined body. If only I could roll like this, in the direction of the British trench, I thought, I could make it back.

Recharged with this thought I started turning over, from back to stomach, in a slow, painful roll, regaining a little of my lost energy on the way. Forcing myself on, I needed to roll over both the dead and the other wounded. Even so, the wounded were unconscious and the dead were past caring. With a sob, I eventually had to stop, it was just too painful to continue.

I was a little further away from the German line, but still well within earshot and rifle shot. Half an hour later, I felt the urge to make another attempt and the slow painful rolling began again. I was now just past the halfway mark, a little closer to the British line than the German line, so at least I was 'sort of' winning.

Suddenly, I caught a glimpse of two people out towards the British wire. It could have been a British or a German raiding party, or the remnants of one returning to base. I noticed as they came closer that they carried a stretcher, but I could see nothing else. By now I had reached a 'give up' stage, I really didn't care, I decided to draw their attention and called quietly. If they were German, I had no hope of life anyway, but if they were British, I had to be careful not to attract the attention of the German sentries, who would have opened fire on them, and me.

At first my call was not audible to them, so I tried again a little louder. They turned and came over to me. Thank God, they were our lads on patrol looking for the wounded survivors. Lifting me carefully, they placed me on the stretcher, then one at each end, they lifted and we were away. Nevertheless, all was not well, something had made the enemy uneasy and they opened up with machine guns. The bearers dropped me to the ground with a bump as they dived for cover, leaving me to roll off the stretcher and back into the mud. The pain from my leg made me feel dizzy, but I remained conscious. My rescuers had made for and were now in, a small shell hole. Lying there in the mud and in some considerable agony, I was delighted that they had saved themselves, for they were now my only hope of a future.

The machine gun finally went quiet, the bearers returned and placed me once more on the stretcher, after which we made another start for home base. We gained about fifty yards this time before the gun opened up once more. For the second time I took a dive to the ground, but this time head first.

The stretcher bearer behind me had been hit, forcing him to lose his end of the carrier. Hell, I thought, I've had it now! We all have. But not so, the wounded bearer got up and he and his partner placed me once more on the carrier and off we went again, the wounded bearer, like the hero he genuinely was, carried on with his duty until I was safely at the back of an old barn, he then went off for his own treatment, helped by his able partner.

The time was now about ten o'clock in the evening. Behind the barn there were hundreds of wounded men waiting for ambulances to arrive. I made certain to call an officer and related to him the sheer guts and bravery of both the stretcher bearers out in the field, particularly the one who carried on although wounded. I also gave him the name and number of this man, which I had obtained as soon as we arrived. The officer wrote it down and I sincerely hope the bearer was in some way rewarded for his courage. He deserved to be, I owed him my life.

We were all now awaiting our turn in the ambulance. In fact I was still waiting some three hours later, but pleased for the chance to be there. The drivers were having a rough time of it but at last my exit was getting closer. The enemy knew the vehicles would be extra busy because they had given us continuous attack, so just to make life more difficult the roads had been heavily shelled. In places, blown away altogether.

Drivers now had to divert and do extra circuits over rough ground. The tactics of warfare are not designed to comply with a gentlemanly code of honour. Kill an enemy and he can be buried and forgotten. Wound many hundreds and you can tie up transport; supplies; medical and surgical services, in the field and at hospital centres, hence, shrapnel shells; antipersonnel traps; gas and the like. It is all a part of wartime strategy.

In our own small Royal Warwickshire part of this attack, we lost eight officers killed, nine officers wounded or missing and over 500 casualties in other ranks, killed, wounded or missing. And yes, they agreed later that carrying out this counter-attack was lamentable, without the efficient support of artillery and without a previous, thorough reconnaissance of the enemy's position.

My turn for transport arrived at about four o'clock in the morning. I was placed into the ambulance with three other wounded men and was at last outward bound. It gave me such great relief and happiness to know that every second drew me further away from the fighting.

It went on without a pause, all around Ypres. Yet again, I recalled the moment of cursing the sergeant major on the Isle of Wight, for not sending me out here quickly enough, big; brave; young; bloody foolish me. Please make this ambulance go faster. Get me away from it God!

A great shell dropped to the rear of us, the driver needed no further encouragement to accelerate. His foot went down to the floor boards and the engine was flat out. There were curses and groans from one of the other chaps with a stomach wound, he had my sympathy, but I was all for the driver and an express service.

At this new speed we soon outdistanced the gunfire and arrived safe and sound at the CCS. There I was given a cup of Bovril and some chocolate, my first food for over twenty-six hours. Up to this point my wound had not been dressed. Out there in the mud unable to sit up for fear of showing movement, my own field dressing pack could not be used, so I guessed I would be in for some considerable discomfort.

The MO started by trying to remove my puttee, now firmly attached to the leg by dried and hardened blood. "It cannot be soaked off," he advised, "Because of the infection risk from the dried mud, we can't chance that getting into the wound, so hold tight." Without further warning, he gripped the fabric and sharply ripped it away. I yelled out, as blood spurted and splashed, but after a thorough cleansing and dressing, I felt so much better and contented. Sleep at last, without disturbance by man, insect, or animal, for the first time in two days.

I had to be awakened by the staff to get into another ambulance that would take a whole crowd of wounded to a railway siding. We were headed for the Base Hospital at Rouen. On arrival there, we were bathed and put into our beds, and joy of joys, attended by English nurses. It was therapeutic just to look at them. I had every reason for being eternally grateful to one Nursing Sister in particular. She came over to me and sat on the side of my bed.

"How old are you?" she asked,

"Nineteen" I replied

"When did you come over to France?"

"Six months ago" I confided, giving her one of my 'little boy lost' looks.

"You poor boy." Her face had a tender maternal expression "You don't look a day older than seventeen, I'll see what I can do to get you on a visit back home!"

She went off to speak to the Medical Officer in charge of the hospital. At the end of the large room, they were in close conversation and the MO turned and looked along the ward in my direction. Sister went on with her duties. Some fifteen minutes later, the MO approached my bed, lifted the medical chart from the clip at the foot and smiled at me whilst adding something to it. He made no comment but turned and walked away.

After he had gone, Sister returned, took the chart and held it out for me to see.

"Well, well, well," she said, her face lighting up with pleasure, "Just look at that."

"It's a red ring." I commented "Does that mean I'm contagious?"

"Just the opposite" she laughed "It just means that you will be on the next boat that leaves for England - Think of me when you get there."

I most certainly did, I never will forget her kindness. Had she not used her influence with the MO on my behalf, I may not have qualified for passing through the base hospital at all. My wound may not have been sufficiently serious. There is something quite irreconcilable about discovering such kindness as this, coupled to a natural love of humanity, amongst so many extreme examples of man's inhumanity to man.

Before leaving here, a captain in the R.War.R was placed next to me whilst we were all being sorted out. Though he seemed to be more badly wounded than I, we were able to hold light conversation. He asked about my battalion and said he had rejoined the Royal Warwick's in September 1914 with a commission to Second Lieutenant, in the 3rd Batt. Service Reserve.

He arrived in France at Ploegsteert in November 1914 and I was delighted to learn that he was now also in the 1st Batt. His promotion to captain as Machine Gun Officer, gave us something in common, other than rank of course. Though he was born in India, the son of an army family, he had grown up in Bishopton, a village I knew in Warwickshire, near Stratford-On-Avon. Being the M.G.Officer he was undeniably pleased to know that I had taken the Machine Gun Course.

I asked him "Did you hear about the incredible Christmas Day gathering with the Germans last year?"

"Yes" he said, "I certainly did, I was at Ploegsteert then, just arrived, what an experience that all was. A second Lt. is not supposed to do such things, but I have this rather strange hobby of collecting buttons. I went out with some of the lads, (to fetch them back of course), and found myself talking to a German Officer. I asked him if he would mind letting me have two buttons off his greatcoat, but he didn't seem to understand, until I took from my coat pocket a pair of wire clippers, and snipped two buttons off the front of his coat. He seemed a little alarmed, but when I snipped two off my own coat and offered them to him, he accepted with a laugh."

I found the captain to be a most interesting man to talk to and it was quite a new experience to find an officer who could accept that an enlisted man was capable of conversation. Regulations however, do make it difficult for officers to fraternise and servicemen appreciate that fact. He was, I discovered later, Captain Bruce Bairnsfather and it was later still, that I learned of his other talents - artist, cartoonist, and journalist, finally to be Official Artist to the War Office. Being a journalist no doubt explained his natural curiosity and enquiring mind, as well as his willingness to converse with the lowly.

He created the 'Ole Bill' cartoon character in the trenches and was a contributor to 'The Bystander' as well as author of 'Bullets and Billets'. Invalided out of the army after recovering from his present wounds, he was appointed Official Cartoonist to the Intelligence Dept. His work was known and loved throughout the UK and many other countries. A brief meeting but

I felt both honoured and privileged to have had such a rare opportunity.

This did bring about the end of my involvement with the Second Battle of Ypres, but the action still continued without me and produced yet another heavy gas attack by the Germans, which occurred on Monday, twenty fourth May, with a repeated strong action the following day.

The German Army had reduced the salient to a small area and achieved their biggest success of that year. They were however, short of men and ammunition, which prevented any major breakthrough taking place. You may well ask - "Was there a cost?" Oh yes! There usually was. During this five week Battle, Germany lost 35,000 men, France lost 10,000 men and British losses, heavier due to the poison gas, amounted to 59,000 men.

"Who passes here?"
"We of the new Brigade, who come in aid - to take your place who fell."
"What is the countersign?"
"That we have weighed the cost ye paid, yet some!"
"Pass! All is well.

Eleven

Recovery at Home

29 April 1915

On the twenty ninth of April, I was carried on board the Hospital Ship 'Carisbrooke Castle.' Departure time having been considerably delayed, I went to sleep and did not wake up until we were outside the docks at Southampton. There we had a short wait for the pilot to come on board and we were efficiently tied up in our berth. Leaving the ship, I was carried, with many others, directly to a waiting Red Cross train and was soon bound for London.

At Paddington Station we were all lined up on our stretchers, the full length of the platform and it was a lengthy platform. Civilians came along giving us cigarettes and chocolate in abundance. They must have found us a touching sight, particularly the more seriously wounded. They simply could not do enough for us.

After a while, an officer approached with a bundle of tallies, attaching one to each patient as if tagging the luggage. He came over to me.

"Where are you from soldier?"

"Birmingham sir" I answered, full of anticipation which thinned down considerably I must admit, when he tied a tally on me for Manchester. I was hoping to have been sent to a Midlands Hospital.

Never mind, I was back in Blighty, away from the slaughter and that was good enough for me. I spent four days in a Manchester Hospital before being sent to Bacup for a period of convalescence. It was a great little place to be. We were taken to a large private house which had been lent to the Government for the purpose of accommodating wounded soldiers. It only held about twenty of us when full and we were the only war wounded in town.

The results could be easily imagined, the local residents made such a fuss of us. We were invited out for free visits to the local cinema, visits to private houses and to local factories for tours and VIP treatment. For those of us able to walk with the aid of sticks or crutches, it was one continuous round of high pleasure.

The people of Bacup were most hospitable and generous. I made a number of good friends there, but nevertheless, I was keen to move on. Having been always something of a rover, with a need for change or a new experience, I now needed to see Liz, my family and folks in Birmingham. I knew I would have to see the doctor about this.

I would have gone to see him there and then, but I had a letter from two old chums, Albert Hill (brother of Freddy) and Jim Boden. They had been told where I was and were making the journey from Birmingham to Bacup by train to see me. That would be wonderful, providing we were allowed visitors, or permitted to go out on our own! I spoke to matron and told her my good news.

"You must remain aware of our policy on town visits, Harry!" She said. "I know what you youngsters are when you get together. You can only go out with them if you give me your word that you will be back here by nine o'clock, sharp." "Yes matron, of course I will, I promise."

The lads arrived and it was so good to see them again. We had such a lot to talk about. They were even able to tell me how well we were doing in the war. It is now quite obvious to me, that the viewpoint held by people over here must relate to another war, most certainly it's not the one I am in!

I made no attempt to tell them what was really happening. They would have suspected me of making it up. I think that some factual reports are now getting through and being published in the papers. It must be said however, that in a paper I saw earlier, it said more about what we were doing to the Germans, than it did about what they were doing to us! We visited a few pubs, and because we were together and I was on crutches in hospital blue, none of us had to buy drinks. The locals did us proud.

Getting rather 'merry,' Jim remarked what a good job the 'No Treating law' had not yet come to pass. It was new to me and I had no idea what he was talking about, I was quite sure it was a leg-pull, however, Albert had read it too. Jim enlarged upon the subject by saying:

"It's perfectly true and if it goes ahead, all the good people in this pub will not be able to provide such hospitality in the future under a new licensing regulation."

"Never," I said, "You're making it up."

"No I'm not" Jim laughed "It intends to go a lot further too. If a man takes his wife out then he can buy her a drink. If she is not his wife, then he has

72

to buy her a meal as well, which will have to be eaten on the premises and not taken away."

"I hope bread and cheese would be acceptable!" piped in Albert between fits of laughter. Jim carried on,

"Bread and cheese might do, but there is another possible let out, it seems that if a lady swoons, she may be 'treated' to brandy by a man" - more laughter.

"Bugger that," I said "not on my pay!"

"Girls often swoon when I take them out," boasted Albert.

"Not surprising," said Jim quickly "it's probably the shock of you offering to buy them *anything*."

True or false we had a grand time and the customers, many of whom joined in the comedy of the subject, enjoyed it too. It was all such a delightful change for me. However, later on I discovered that it was true. A 'No treating' law was being discussed in the Commons. The whole strange idea was to be applied to the London Metropolitan area only, if accepted. I should have been pleased to know that our politicians were keeping themselves busy, but I wasn't.

At midnight, I returned to the Hospital, sneaked in and crept along the corridor, I had got as far as the main hall, where I found matron waiting for me. She was not a happy lady and scolded me for going back on my word. The next morning she escorted me into the doctor's office on reprimand.

This didn't appear to be the appropriate time to ask him if I could be discharged, so I decided to let that rest until my bad behaviour had been forgotten. "Matron has told me all about your escapade," he began, "I agree with her that you have totally overstepped the mark. You must remember why you are here. Our efforts to help you recover are wasted if we cannot get your whole hearted co-operation. There are others that I feel are more deserving and therefore I am discharging you. That's all, you may go."

I forced a serious look on my face, but my delight at this was immense. Immediately I started writing letters home to tell everyone that I would soon be with them on sick leave and what time and day I would be leaving Bacup. That done, I went out to post the letters and visit the houses of Bacup friends, to give them the news.

Almost every house brought out a bottle of Scotch whisky and poured me a glass. We toasted the present, our health, the future, our families, the cat, the dog, and anything else we could think of. I then had to wobble on my three unsteady legs, back to the Hospital.

Clattering through the door as quietly as I could manage, down the corridor and into the main hall, I met once more, dear old matron. "Oh! - its

73

you Harry," she said, then observing my condition, she patted a chair as she said, "Sit down here, I want to talk to you." She did. I had the full benefit of her opinion, which I am quite sure I deserved and she was entitled to give. I don't think it changed me at all though, for in my state at that time, I failed to take-in, or even remember a single word she said, however I am sure she meant well, bless her. I was being most unreasonable, in view of their kindness.

The journey home was uneventful, except for one strange occurrence. I needed to change trains at Manchester and await the one to Birmingham. My head was filled with the sheer joy and warmth of returning for a visit back home. After my last ordeal of battle, I had given up all hope of ever getting there. Suddenly, right out of the blue, a young girl of about nineteen approached me.

"Hello," she began "Can you help me?"

"In what way," I asked, hesitating more than just a little?"

"I have nowhere to go," she said.

Oh dear I thought, what's this leading to, surely they haven't started to allow the freedom of the rail stations for prostitution in my absence?

"I really don't think I can help you, in any way at all," I said, "And what is more, I have no money!" That should fix her.

"I am not asking you for money! I thought you could help me."

I tried another question "In what way do you think I can help you?"

It has to be admitted, I had felt safer than this when in No-Man's-Land and I was wishing she had chosen someone else.

"I thought perhaps you could take me home with you, or wherever you are going."

I was completely dumbfounded, almost speechless, I tried to imagine the scene, "Hello mum, here I am at last, meet my new homeless friend who has no place to go, can she stay here with you, when I go back?" Or to Liz, "Hello Liz, this girl means nothing to me, it was just that she had no place to go!" It took me ten minutes to shake her off! It would appear that she had only just arrived as a Belgian refugee, so I suggested she went to a police station. I think they would have put her in the right direction.

The train that carried me to Birmingham arrived rather later than anticipated, but was met by a crowd of relatives. We all had to walk home because the last Tram-car had been put to bed some hours ago. They gave me a small bottle of Scotch to help my journey, but there were a lot of us. Passing it around, the bottle was empty before the journey was any more than halfway completed.

It was good to be back and excellent news to hear that my five brothers were still going strong - all at the front and somewhere in France or Belgium. Sadly my seven days went by so quickly that I was soon saying goodbye once more. With so many people to see, it was a pity only to spend such a short time with Liz. We did enjoy the time we had though. In fact she showed me a letter she had received from one of her brothers.

"It's a pity you haven't had a chance to meet Jim and Harry out there, I'm sure you would get on well with them," she said.

"The two of them have joined up together haven't they?" I questioned

"Yes, in the Seaforth Highlanders. In fact they are both in the same battalion in France.

"But, surely they're Brummies?"

"Yes! And mum's Irish and dad was in the Argyll and Sutherland's, what difference does that make?" I laughed and said "Well, with that sort of mixture, how could they refuse to take Jim and Harry in the Seaforths. As long as the other Seaforths don't object."

"Oh!" Liz replied with a smile, I don't think they would complain too loudly, Jim is their boxing champion."

My changed expression turned her smile to laughter.

"Do you know," I said, "We do have a battalion of Seaforths in my Division. In fact, at one of our training sessions at Oultersteene in early April, we played them at football, and we won 4-0. What Field address do you put on their letters?"

"This;" she held out an envelope, "And I think they are in the 2nd battalion."

"Well, of course I can't promise but I can make enquiries and see if they are within reach at any time!"

"Oh good, if you are going back to the same area again, it would be lovely if you could pop in and say

James Rogers (Father of Liz) Argyll & Sutherland Highlanders Regt.

75

Hal Rogers

hello, I have told them about you and that you are out there."

This was almost unbelievable, the thought of me 'popping' out for the afternoon to visit friends in the trenches.

"Just keep the war going for me chaps, I'll be back soon!" Laughter seemed to be the only response. Liz looked surprised,

"You do mean it, don't you, I mean you will look them up if they are in your group?"

"Division," I corrected. "Yes! But you will bear in mind won't you, that I don't get time off in the front line, any more than they do. Also, with something like half a million men out there, I shall have to go out and ask "Hey! Any of you fellers know Jim and Harry Rogers, two Brummie Scots?"

We both began laughing at the situation and it was a happy note on which to say our goodbyes. I then left for Southampton and the Isle of Wight. Reporting first to the Guardroom and then to the sergeant major, the same one that I had cursed for not sending me out sooner. Recognising me, his face spread into a broad grin,

"So! You came back then, fun was it? Have a good time did you?"

"No," I answered, "It wasn't - and I didn't, you should have persuaded me not to go?"

"What?" he said, after all the moaning you put in about missing it all, I would never have dreamed of spoiling your fun, but I'm glad to see you made it back OK." We chatted a little about the experience, after which we shook hands and he directed me to the GTC or Gradual Training Company.

This was a sort of rehabilitation unit, to get us fit to go out again. The local nickname was the 'Flying Corps' because of the speed at which we moved. My first march was a slow affair being unable to maintain balance. In fact everyone was walking in slow motion, half of the men had sticks and

'Big Jim' Rogers with two sisters, Liz on left and Louise on right (of picture)

limped along, although I learned that few of them had leg wounds, and some had been there for much longer than they needed.

 One week of this was enough for me. I asked if I could be transferred to the Training Company. I was happier there, although the training was hard. I would not pretend to be injured just to extend the soft option and remain at the GTC.

If the Sergeant steals your rum never mind
If the Sergeant steals your rum never mind
Though he's just a rotten sot, let him take the bloody lot
If the Sergeant steals your rum never mind

Twelve

11th Battalion R.War.R - *In France*

July 1915

During the month of July, I wouldn't say that I was open to it, but the sergeant major set a roguish trap for me. Never trust a sergeant major! We had been out digging trenches (for practice, just what I needed!) on the top of the Downs when he approached us with the comment

"I want ninety six B.E.F men to join up with the 11th battalion, they are only half trained and won't be going out to France for a long time yet. They are in need of an experienced element within their battalion and most of you chaps would be ideal for them. Any volunteers?"

Being in no hurry to get back across the channel I quickly answered,

"Put me down if they are not going yet"

"Fine, they are only half trained, as I said, so it will be quite a long time before they can go, you will be all right with them." Did I detect a slight grin as he said it? Maybe not, but he had an unusual expression on his sergeant major type face.

He got all ninety six of his men and we joined our new battalion which was stationed at Ludgershall on the Salisbury Plain. When we arrived we were naturally inspected by their colonel, who delivered the usual preliminary 'getting to know you' speech, which followed the usual track: "I want you men to thoroughly understand, that you are not coming here to ruin the present discipline of my battalion. I know only too well what you Expeditionary Force men are like and if I have any trouble with you, especially in France, I shall have no hesitation in having you shot - Please understand that well."

What was it with all these bloody colonels? Why did they all feel the need to get co-operation by going around threatening to shoot everyone? With

79

colonels like some of ours, who the hell needed an enemy? How easy it is to be verbally courageous. Omar Khayyám was surely right, *"Oh the brave beating of a distant drum."* He must have met a few of our top brass.

You may well ask what happened to the jolly jape of the SM. Well, after exactly TWO DAYS at Ludgershall, we were setting sail for France. I thought he wore a funny expression, the scheming toad. My feelings were understandably different this time. I was not quite so raw as on the first visit. Gone was the boyish excitement that I once felt. It was no adventure now.

I had no worries previously, whereas now, my great concern was simply, that we were going to France. There was the stark and blinding light of full knowledge. I knew what it was all about and what it was like. That same knowledge, previously lacking, had now become a disadvantage. I felt young enough in body at nineteen and a half, but a good deal older than that in mind and experience. Grin and bear it, I resolved. I could blame no one. At least if I went down I would make sure I did not shame my comrades or my family. The enemy wouldn't find me easy to take, or to dispatch.

On the boat once more, I watched from the stern as England faded into the mist on the horizon. How I loved that country. Two hours or so later I saw the approach of French shores. There was plenty of excitement from the large numbers of the battalion who were on their first visit. The Expeditionary 'ninety-six' did not share their enthusiasm. There was no fuss

made by the local population either when we landed in France. The event had latterly become rather common- place and taken for granted.

We quietly disembarked, formed up and marched off to the same old base camp, where we were issued with a blanket, which could be guaranteed to be lousy before tomorrow morning. Sure enough it was, the next day was spent doing the old scratching exercises and once more I was lousy as an old rook.

Liz. A small cameo picture taken by Seaman's Studios, Birmingham, to send to Harry while he was away.

We had all learned to recognise 'Trench Foot' now and I think even the officers appreciated that the cause was trench water, (which I remember only too well) though whether or not they still regard taking a boot off as a crime I don't know. As if we hadn't enough to contend with, another malady was now rising to become a problem, that was 'Trench Fever' spread by those damned lice.

We did not spend much time at the base. The battalion was ordered to march towards the firing line within a couple of days of its arrival in France. An average of twenty miles each day, then a little help by way of a few hours in a train and we were getting nearer to our dugout homes and the unfriendly (or perhaps as a colleague put it, hun-friendly) rats.

A few more forced marches and we were there, waiting for our turn in the trenches. That night we slept in a barn, so I made my bed early and got into it. No good gaining experience unless it's put into practice! I knew that for the next twelve days the longest period for sleeping would be three hours, at intervals.

The following morning (feeling right up to scratch) with buttons and bayonet shining, and boots highly polished, we had a platoon drill session, followed by bayonet practice. It always seemed strange to think that one day I might have to spear someone with the bayonet. It polished well, and we had plenty of practice killing sacks of straw, but I somehow could not imagine actually sticking it in a living man.

The weapons were quite long, 17 inches of single edged, sharpened steel. More like a short sword really, with a long groove to act as a 'blood let' or 'fuller' the sole purpose of this, being to aid penetration and extraction. It clipped to the end of our Lee Enfield rifles, to give the reach of a spear or lance. After dismissal, I went with a few old soldiers and we found a small 'Estaminet' where we enjoyed a few beers to give us cheer for the afternoon parade.

We succeeded so well, that standing still and upright on parade was the hardest task of the day. Only marching to the trench that night with a splitting headache, was marginally worse. I really didn't care if a million shells were lobbed at us.

An interesting feature, as we neared the front line, was the addition of new communication trenches. Many of us were delighted to see them, wisdom at last, a really fine idea. We can now get to our forward trench, which is within about two hundred yards of the German trench, under full cover, providing we keep low. No more do we need to leave one trench to walk over the top to another.

There was a stronger system developing and the typical layout became three lines, 'front - support - and reserve,' these trenches were about seven feet deep and were being linked by the communication system. Not as much protection given as the line trenches, but a great idea, which meant no more wurzel fields.

At the forward (front) trench, the sergeants posted their sentries. Not surprisingly, all the men selected for first duty on the firing step were BEF men, who had been out there before and had experience. It was a quiet night, so we didn't mind too much. Throughout the night, I never heard a single shot fired within a thousand yards of us.

Things were so quiet that when our first duty was completed, my co-sentry, a fellow private named Percy Lackey, suggested that we went out into No-Man's-Land on a patrol. I was game and we approached the platoon officer.

"Good God, No!" He said in horror "If you were hit or anything happened, how could we possibly get you back, I will speak to the captain, but there is no way he could agree to that I am sure."

He did speak to the captain, who obviously knew the strength of the situation more so than the young platoon officer and thought it an excellent idea, providing we took an NCO with us and made it a patrol for gaining 'intelligence' of the enemy position, attitude and probable strength. An experienced NCO was located and word was passed up and down the line, 'Three men are going out on patrol so don't fire at movement.'

We left the trench over the sandbags on the parapet and crawled stomach to the ground over No-Man's-Land, towards the German trenches. Extra care was needed because at this stage we did not know exactly where they were. Having reached the halfway distance, a strange yet familiar stench hit our nostrils. A few yards more and the source was discovered. It was the rotting body of a German soldier that had been there for a considerable time. Percy wanted to drag him back to our trench but the NCO would not hear of it. We carried on with our slow journey and stopped when we reached the German wire. There, we lay still and watched their activities.

After about an hour, we saw that a party of them had gathered and they were themselves, preparing to mount their parapet to come out into No-Man's-Land. We knew better than to wait around and greet them. Going into a reversal of our outward trip, we followed our approach track and crawled backwards, the way we had come.

At the halfway point once more, we again met the dead German. We looked forward and could now see the equipment carried by the outgoing

Typical Trench Section

Parados   Parados

Parapet of sandbags   Traverse   Parapet of sandbags
fire step   9' x 9'   fire step

3' | 12'

Latrine | Urinal

Steps or Ramp

A section drawing of a typical Trench layout of the period, showing facilities and the essential 'Traverse' which was placed at intervals, to prevent invaders charging through to take the occupants by storm.

German party. It was obvious that their only concern was to add to their own wire. A few nods and movements of the head from my partner and we relieved the body of it's rifle and other equipment, without telling the NCO of course, before continuing our reverse crawl to our own trench.

We delivered our booty, with some pride, to the platoon officer, who was livid. "That is a disgusting thing to do" he cried, "A totally pointless and futile recovery of objects from the dead." He paused, then snapped out, "Take them back at once!"

"Beg your pardon, sir?"

"You heard me, take them back where you found them, right now, that's an order."

Not a lot of choice after that, Percy and I once more mounted the parapet and a patrol of two went out to return the dead man's equipment.

"Perhaps they think he might need it to take with him when he reports to The 'Big CO' in the sky" Percy muttered as we crawled out. At the first opportunity we dropped it all in a shell hole and crawled back.

Volunteering for that patrol to break the monotony, proved to be not such a good idea. Percy and I were now both marked men. The officers, pleased to have someone on hand who apparently enjoyed their work, gave us plenty of opportunity.

One of us seemed to be selected to join every damn patrol or bombing raid that the company took part in. Our experience grew rapidly. Percy and I worked well together, we seemed to be kindred spirits and we enjoyed being together on these excursions.

After being with regulars throughout my service up to now, I found it strange being with a battalion that had absolutely no experience of warfare. To give an example of this, on one particular day, Percy and me were sitting on the firing step, with our hats off, when the platoon officer approached through the trench.

His buttons glistened, with tiny pin points of light, radiating star reflections, his boots held a polish such as could only be seen in some advert for Cherry Blossom or Kiwi. In fact he looked as if he had stepped directly from a London taxi.

One look at the two of us was all he needed.

"Put your hats on at once, even in the firing line you must be properly dressed." Well, we enjoyed the joke and had to laugh. He wasn't joking however and in return for our laughter, we were ordered to get a couple of brooms and sweep the trenches. Who before that day had ever heard of such a thing? Here we were, in France, sweeping out the bloody trenches.

We also had to take up the boards covering the sump holes and clean the sumps out! After complaining and moaning at him to his face I said,

"I hope it rains, then all the trenches will fall in, and you can trade in your brooms for a dredger." That amused him and all the other B.E.F. men in the area, but we still had to carry on sweeping and cleaning.

On the wall, on the wall
Whiter than the whitewash on the wall,
Wash me in the water that you wash your dirty daughter in
and I shall be whiter than the whitewash on the wall

Thirteen

To Take Prisoners

Late August 1915

For several weeks we had a really quiet time of it and under such circumstances as this, it is difficult to keep a whole company of men occupied. The CO found his own solution to the problem by deciding it was time for a bombing raid on the German trenches.

The object, we understood, being to capture a few prisoners and send them to Brigade HQ. The men selected for this raid (of course) included my partner in crime, the NCO and me, the eager volunteers for the first patrol. The full compliment was one officer, two NCOs, and eight privates, from my company, assisted by four Royal Engineers.

White tapes were put out as we went, for this had to be a lightning raid making a surprise attack. The tape would guide us back when we made our return. With faces and hands blackened, to reduce our visibility to the enemy, at eleven thirty pm, we entered the saphead, (entrance to our covered siege trench or 'SAP', dug out by the Sappers of course), from which all official attacks and raids began. Creeping out, we re-formed as near the German lines as we could possibly get without raising the alarm by being seen.

We waited for the scheduled and prearranged 'box barrage,' to be sent over by our Artillery. This would effectively cut off and isolate the part of the enemy trench we intended attacking, and would prevent interference with our purpose. Zero, zero and the guns blazed, spewing their deadly shells over the first area, smashing the German wire in front of us, to facilitate our rapid and unhindered progress.

The guns were then elevated on each side, to cave-in both ends of the trench to be attacked, isolating those particular occupants of the centre section. Blocking their communication with both ends of their trench. Our artillery then adjusted the elevation of all the guns once more, to pound the second and third line trenches of the enemy, driving them further back still and pushing their reserves further away, in order to give us a little more time. This was the purpose of a box barrage.

The second the guns stopped, our officer was on his feet and dashing through the large gap in the wire, the remainder of the patrol hot on his heels. Then followed a rare stroke of absolute luck. As we leapt into the shortened trench sector, two German soldiers who were caught out and were now on their own in the trench, immediately threw their hands up into the air.

"Two men take these prisoners back into our Lines" shouted our officer "Now wait!"

The two men went off with the German soldiers as instructed and so far half our work had been done. The CO had got his prisoners but now came the bombing raid. This was where the Engineers came in. They raced down the remainder of the trench and dropped into each dugout they came to, a trench mortar bomb. From down below we could hear the screams of the trapped men in their pre-death panic. They must have identified the objects as bombs just as the explosives ripped apart their only shelter, converting it to a tomb.

"Back," came our officer's cry, "Back- for your damned lives." We were certainly not keen to hang about after that and all members of the party practically flew over the parapet of the German trench. We looked for the man we had left by the gap in the German wire, as a guide just for this particular moment then retraced the tapes. By this time, although it had been a rapid affair the enemy reaction was much in evidence.

German artillery opened up and so did their machine guns. God those German machine guns are deadly weapons. There certainly did not appear to be a shortage of them in the enemy lines. We dared not stop but just kept going on, until we came to our barbed wire. Struggling through this we dived head first into our own trench.

A quick roll call confirmed that we had suffered no casualties and therefore the raid was a complete success, from our point of view, that is! From initial box barrage to the head first dive back into our trench, we were timed at exactly twelve minutes.

We were excused further duties for the remainder of the night and received a double issue of rum to help us sleep. This was appreciated but sleep was next to impossible for any of us. We were at the receiving end of German gunfire all night long and the shells they sent over practically smashed our trench in. Digging it out again would have to be our first job in the morning.

During the next period of rest outside the front line, I was asked by the captain for the third time, if I would consider promotion. I had previously refused, but this time accepted and became 'Lance Corporal Morgan.' The captain went on to say, "Tell me, are you not a trained machine gunner?"

"Yes sir," I replied, "With a first class pass."

"Well done, that will be useful, I hope they instructed on the Lewis gun?"

"Yes sir they did, but the concentration was on the Vickers, being heavier and more effective."

"Interesting" the captain said "That explains it then, you see we are to receive a number of Lewis guns in the battalion, four, I think. The CO raised a preference for Vickers rather than Lewis but we understand that all present Vickers guns are being diverted to the new 'Machine Gun Corps' being formed sometime in October this year. What you tell me is interesting. That's all; thank you, corporal"

"Thank you sir," I saluted, turned and walked back along the trench. So, I was now a lance corporal; I bet the sergeant armourer at the Machine Gun Course was delighted with the news about the new Corps of MGs. But it seems he was right about one thing, still limited supplies of 'Vickers' per battalion.

I shall be lucky if I ever see a machine gun again, let alone fire one. However, if the captain is right with his information, at least we shall have four. Not quantity enough to frighten the Germans too much, but an improvement nevertheless. Hell; four for each battalion! Let's hope they can afford to include a few spare belts of ammo.

Fourteen

Bombing School Training Course

October 1915

My reward for accepting promotion? Oh yes, I was rewarded. I was sent on a seven day training course at a bombing school. The school was a considerable distance behind the front lines and I have to admit, I found it exciting. It covered everything presently available, including the early-in the-war improvised missiles, made by the troops from jam and tobacco tins, when hostilities began last year.

Now the munitions factories were in gear however, there was no shortage of the real thing. Mass production began this year (1915) and the anti personnel grenade adopted as standard by the British Army was the Mills bomb. Hale's grenades had been adopted some time ago for rifle use, they had a four ounce explosive charge in a brass tube, enclosed in a cast-iron ring and they fragmented on detonation. A thin steel rod protruding from the base, had to be inserted into the rifle barrel, which served to stabilise and guide the missile when fired. The bomb itself exploded upon impact.

As our MG instructor would have said, "There is a slight disadvantage however." His 'slight disadvantages' were always major issues, and in this case the steel rod, it would seem, damaged the rifling inside the rifle barrel put there to induce a spin to the fired bullet, the steel rod soon destroyed accuracy, making that rifle useless for its designed purpose. Rifles used for the launching of Hale's grenades therefore had to be set aside, specifically for that purpose.

We concentrated on and practised with the Mills. A small pineapple shaped, cast-iron segmented little chap, which sat well in the palm of the hand. It had a spring-loaded lever, held by a ringed split-pin and you had just five seconds in which to dispose of the bomb, after pulling the pin. We practised throwing them, with dummy models and then live. It was great fun and I enjoyed every minute of it. Once more I was delighted to receive a 'First Class Bombing Squad Leader' pass.

From that time I practically lived in No-Man's-Land. On every patrol, on every raid, on every covering party to protect the barbed wire men, I was there. Frequently I was on the point of telling them what they could do with their stripe! Wet weather had once more set-in with a vengeance. The trenches had begun to fall in and collapse all along the line. Dugouts were half full of thick, sticky, mud and only the deep trenches appeared to have escaped the collapse. Deeper ones had held firm and dry, but the others were impossible to rest in. The sergeant major had the deepest and therefore the best - guess who had the remainder!

The lads were frequently stuck in the mud, and when others went to help them dig out, they themselves became stuck. Our only mild consolation was that the Germans hopefully, had the same problems.

On countless occasions, we had to dash down the trench with our spades to where a dug out had collapsed and buried some of the men. It could be the rain loosening the soil, or the vibration of the constant bombardments, or a combination of both. Working fast we could save a lot of them from suffocation, but we lost quite a few.

We were happy to be relieved for a few days behind the lines, but the euphoria was short lived. The trench situation had become so bad that we were marched back every day, some five or six miles, to try and clear out some of the mud, a totally hopeless task. We would dig it out and could see it refilling as we worked.

It stuck, it sucked and it stank. Consequently, after a hard day spent digging out, we had this march back to billets to look forward to. By the time we got back to the barn, most of us simply dropped to the floor in our equipment, too weak and shattered to pull it off. Some mongrel dogs were better looked after than this and to the folks back home we were their fighting heroes. They didn't know the half of it!

A happy day followed, it was pay day. As soon as my ten francs were in my hands I made a beeline for the nearest Estaminet. It was crowded out with our troops. All was lively, with a piano churning out all the presently popular tunes. My whole ten francs were happily disposed of in that cheery environment.

I always made a habit of spending everything I had before going back into the trenches, and had good reason for it, I never knew if I would make it through the day, or be taken prisoner, and if I wasn't going to spend the money, I made damn sure that no Germans did. I could imagine them taking the pay out of my pocket and enjoying a laugh over a bottle of beer. "Ere is to ze poor Englander svine, who lost his pay." So I drank a pleasant toast to my own health instead.

After that I returned to my bed, which had now been modified by the addition of some wire netting from the old barn. It was a lovely break. I wondered what my brothers, and Fred were all doing and where about in France they were.

What a laugh if we bumped into each other in an Estaminet one day, all of them, at the same time. I could see it now, the door of the bar opening and one by one they would make an entrance, Jack leading them through would say "Hello Perch, how are you," and after my brothers were in, Fred would be the last to arrive, wheeling two bikes, "Come on Harry its training time," then I remembered no more sleep took over!

Next morning, back to the trenches, franc-less. I gathered my bombing squad and we made off towards the communication trench. What a ghastly mess it was in, three feet of mud and water to wade through, slipping and sliding all over the place. We managed reasonably well and I led them along to a point where I saw a duckboard floating. I pushed it out of my path and stepped forward, only to plunge feet first into a seven foot deep sump hole, where I disappeared from their view.

Fortunately, I had a quick reaction and drew a deep breath before I went down. Being a good swimmer I was accustomed to the feeling of being submerged, but not by this filthy water. My eyes were tightly shut and I thought to myself "Christ almighty, what a way to go, not killed in battle, but lost down a bloody sump hole."

Of course I should have guessed that the duckboard covered something. There was nothing I could do about it. I had my rifle slung around my neck, was in full marching order, carrying many rounds of ammunition and loaded bomb pouches. There was no chance of floating, or getting out without help. Suddenly I felt a clonk as something hit my steel helmet from above. Still with eyes tightly shut, I raised an arm and found something to take hold of. By this time my lungs felt ready to burst.

It was only the quick thinking of my bomber team, who poked their rifles down the hole for me to grab, that saved me from drowning. They pulled me out, with only 'light' merriment. They were easily amused!

We continued our soggy journey and passed the word back "Mind the sump hole." However, as the sump was under water and the duckboard had now floated well away from it, one out of every ten took a dive.

All night long the rain pelted down, as we waited on 'standby' in the communications trench. I stood under a sheet of corrugated iron in my sodden clothing, listening to the patter of tiny feet as the rats scuttled about, crossing the trench over the top of my shelter. It was cause for alarm how big these rats were growing. Their new environment provided an abundance of horse and human flesh, rotting and decaying over a vast area. They were clearly proliferating and growing horribly.

By dawn the next day, my condition was pitiful, frozen to the bone and teeth chattering uncontrollably. The platoon officer looked at me and said,

"Clean that rifle." That man was getting right up my nose. My reaction was instinctive and I told him in plain English what he could do with the rifle. In fact perhaps too plain because I found myself once more up for orders.

It must be a sign however, that my experience, and the fact of mixing with all the regulars is paying off, because instead of getting into the panic of previous instances, I went at once to my company captain. I showed him the dreadful state I was in at that moment, and explained the ordeal of the duty just completed. This was followed by an apology, for my comments to the platoon officer, which, I said, were uttered during a moment of exceptional stress. It worked: by God, it worked, the case was dismissed and I was allowed to dry my clothing by the stove in the captain's dugout.

The bells of hell go ting-aling-aling, for you but not for me
And the little girls all sing-aling-aling, for you but not for me
Oh death where is thy sting-aling-aling or grave thy victory
The bells of hell go ting-aling-aling, for you but not for me

Fifteen

A Patrol I Missed

December 1915

Tonight a patrol would be going out into No-Man's-Land and an instruction was issued that there would be no combat unless absolutely necessary. There would be a sergeant, corporal and nine men. The sergeant selected his numbers and included Percy Lackey, my mate.

When I saw this, I asked if I could be added to the list as well.

"Sorry," he said, "I've got my quota." I did my best to press him further,

"You mean to say one more will make a difference?" However, he was authorised for one corporal and he had one.

I found Percy and complained,

"How come you were selected for this one and not me? You know bloody well that without me to look after you, you'll take a wrong turning and get lost."

"They know who their best men are" he replied with a smile, "I told them to leave you behind this time as you would only get in the way."

"Rotten sod" I chided as we shook hands, "Mind how you go, and don't do anything daft, I shall be on the lookout for you and I'll open the front door when you get back."

"Yes dad," he laughed, "But don't wait up."

Ten thirty pm and the patrol moved out, I watched them go through our wire and disappear into the blackness of No-Man's-Land. I had such an indescribable feeling about them that I remained on the firing step at the side of one of the sentries, listening and watching. I had never felt so much on edge. I simply sensed that something would happen.

Something did happen, at eleven fifteen I could hear the bursting explosions of bombs and the sharper crack of rifle fire. It lasted for about two minutes before all was once again silent. The patrol should now come scampering back. I waited, but it didn't. Slowly the hours dragged by and still, nothing.

An officer came up to ask me the question in everyone's mind,

"Anyone returned yet Corporal?"

"No sir! I don't think any of them will. They are all well trained, experienced men, and if they were alive they would be here by now."

"I think they are just laying low," he muttered as he walked away, but nevertheless, not one of them came back. It was at least two months later when we learned that four of them had survived and been taken prisoner. One of the four wrote to a colleague and explained:

"As we went out, we were observed by a much stronger German patrol. When we moved forward, the Germans swung around behind us, threw their bombs and opened up with a rapid fire. Of our eleven man unit, we had seven killed and four taken prisoner." Percy Lackey was not one of them - he was dead. If the sergeant major had taken notice of me, I feel quite sure that I would have died with him. Fate had allocated a killed list of eight and I felt that I had double-crossed my pal, by not being with him on that occasion. This was the only patrol I had ever missed in my company and none came back.

A short time after this, we moved to another part of the line called Hennescamps (north of Gommecourt). There would be a great deal of patrol work needed here, finding gaps in the German wire amongst other tasks. Our main route was the Essart Road which ran through our lines and then on through the enemy lines. It was a splendid guide for us in the dark and it lessened the danger of walking into the wrong trench.

One particularly exciting event on this road took place after I heard muffled bumps from where I stood on the firing steps. They came from the German end. I was still listening intently when Sergeant de St Croix, the Battalion Bombing Sergeant came along. I waved an arm to beckon him to me, saying,

"Just come and listen to this sergeant, what do you think it is?"

We both stood there and he suddenly murmured,

"The Germans are working on a barricade across the road, get six Mills bombs, we will go out and move them on." I went off to get the bombs thinking to myself 'Well Morgan, you have done it again, you know what a demon for fighting this sergeant is, now you are going with him.' It was true he was an exceptionally brave man and also an expert with bombs, his favourite weapon.

Of the six bombs selected, I gave him three and kept three for myself.

"Take your equipment off," he instructed "Put the bombs in your pockets."

This I did and the word was passed - left and right - that two men were going out in front. We quietly crossed our wire, the sergeant with his Mk.VI Webley revolver in his left hand and a Mills bomb in the right. Making directly for the road, we advanced carefully towards the German working party keeping close to the left hand bank.

Just one hundred and fifty yards from our own trench and we could see the enemy quite clearly, working on their project.

"We'll get a little closer," the sergeant whispered and we slowly moved forward a further fifty yards or so. He then nodded in my direction and we threw all six bombs into the pack of workers.

There must have been a great many casualties if the shouts, screams and groans were any guide. The Mills bombs exploded and fragmented, spreading a blanket of shrapnel over a wide area. Those that could manage it, made a dash for their own trench, leaving the wounded for the time being to take care of themselves. I knew that feeling well!

For the present my instinctive impulse was to turn back and run for our trench. In fact, had it not been for the cool thinking of Sergeant de St Croix, I probably would have done just that. "Follow me corporal" he said and on hands and knees we crept along the German wire, in the opposite direction to the road.

It became evident at that point, that the road was being strafed by machine gun fire. Had we gone back the same way that we entered, we would have been wiped out completely. The sergeant explained his reasoning and it was quite clear that he was right. After this experience, I was fully aware of the professional efficiency of this man. I trusted him and without hesitation would have followed him anywhere.

Finding a deep shell hole, we both jumped in and sat there waiting for the excitement to settle.

"We have to be patient now corporal, until things cool down a bit, then we can go back."

"How about if any of them come out to look around?" I asked.

A slight pause, before he answered "Pray that they don't!" Then seeing the wry smile on my face and slight shrug of my shoulders, he added "Not a religious man then Harry?"

"I find it difficult to think of God being with us in this war, when he seems to be giving so much help to the Germans." I replied. It was now his turn to smile as he said,

"Maybe God feels that he is responsible for everyone, and must be equally fair to all his children!"

"Then, he should stop sitting on the fence and come down to tell one of us we are wrong."

"I wonder" the sergeant reflected, "if perhaps, he just thinks that putting us here and giving us the benefit of intelligence, we should be able to work that out for ourselves?"

"We can hardly do that," I answered, "because we have leaders with the authority to make decisions for us. We don't have the right to make a judgement of our own, and act on it without their consent." He chuckled softly saying,

"Then we can't blame dear old God for that, can we? If we permit it to happen, it must be our fault, or the fault of our leaders, and they were appointed by a system we accepted! One or the other."

I felt he was wrapping me up in this conversation and I was running out of counterpoints, I tried a last stab.

"Then maybe God's biggest mistake was in putting us here on earth with a greater intelligence than other animals!" I persisted.

"I'll grant you, there is something to be said for that," he replied. "Though in all honesty I have met many people whose intelligence level would rate far lower than some animals." He paused, "Is there something worrying you Harry?" This was like a bolt out of the blue to me. I did have a problem, but thought that it was disguised.

"Well! Since you ask, there is something that does concern me sergeant" I confided, "I feel unsettled about all these people dying every day, I know as a soldier it has to happen, but there is far more killing than I ever imagined and I find it hard to take. I try to look cool calm and collected, but inside, it scares me."

"That's quite another matter, but **you** have to work that out, and the sooner the better Harry, but let's keep it quiet, we still don't know who's out there" he said, in a hushed voice. I moved closer, digging my heels further into the wall of mud, though with the guns still firing and shells bursting, it seemed a little strange to expect anyone to overhear us.

We sat silent for a short time before he turned his head towards me, tipping it forward to look thoughtfully at the bottom of the shell hole.

"Which men do you have a problem with, theirs or ours?"

"Is there any difference?"

"Of course there is," he said seriously, "Those on our side are our comrades, though the less you know about them, the better. All the others are the enemy. You have to get into the habit of thinking that way Harry, it's the only way to justify being here and the only way you will survive. Look at it this way, a lot of people like to eat meat, but only a relative few could work in an abattoir.

Think of us as policemen bringing in an international band of criminals. Any that resist arrest, we are empowered to shoot. When their leaders are caught they will be tried as criminals and sentenced. The enemy know this and being soldiers themselves, accept the situation, as we do. That after all, is why we became soldiers in the first place.

We are now engaged in a war, the like of which few of us could have imagined, let alone seen, trained to work in what is fast becoming some sort of open slaughter house. However, to the German, WE are the enemy. If you hesitate to kill him, he will certainly not hesitate to kill you.

There will come a time when you have to make fast a decision on this point, your response will need to be instinctive, and pausing to think about it, could cost you your life! As far as your comrades are concerned, think of them only as that, not as your friends, that will do them no good, or yourself either!" He moved his head to face me. That, Harry, is our penalty for being soldiers."

He stayed looking at me, to get eye-to-eye contact, saying,

"Don't be afraid of fear, Harry, we all have it. Be suspicious of anyone who claims to be immune, they could be a danger. It's fear that keeps us alert and on our toes, it keeps us sharp and watchful, a degree of fear is necessary. What we do not want, and must try to avoid at all cost, is panic. Panic is destructive!"

He paused and lifted his head to listen. The firing had now stopped.

"Come on," he whispered, "I'm sorry Harry, I didn't mean to give you a lecture, but I hope it helps a little, we can go back now."

We climbed out of our shelter and made it back to our own lines. There we followed standard practice by first reporting our return to the sentries. It must have been about half an hour later, when an officer came to me saying,

"I have had the sergeants report and he tells me you did some good work tonight corporal. You are excused all further duties until stand-to in the morning."

"Thank you sir," I said, and paused before asking him "Have you ever been out on a raid, with Sergeant de St Croix, sir?" Smiling at my youthful audacity, he replied,

"No, I can't say that I have, and neither can I say that I'm extra keen to, though if I do go out in the near future, he is one man I would prefer to have with me. How did you enjoy his company on your outing?"

"Well sir, an hour or two out there with him certainly raises your helmet about six inches. I think I've now aged to about 35 years old. But apart from that I think I am also now a bit wiser." He smiled as he turned and walked off down the trench.

For all my thoughts about the patrol just completed, I had no idea of the nightmare about to follow, or the fact that the sergeant's words to me would be put to the test so soon. It was perhaps, just as well!

Sixteen

FULL TIME ACTOR

March 1916

Lance Corporal, 'acting' corporal, not even a full corporal, I had now also been placed, due to my unique experience, as 'acting' company bombing sergeant heading up the bomber team of my own "A" company, whose captain now came over to me whilst I was still in the trench.

"B company are going out tonight on a fighting patrol corporal. They have requested to borrow you in reserve, in case their own bombing sergeant gets knocked over. Do you wish to volunteer for it?"

I was now beginning to get more than a little worried by the attention I seemed to be attracting. My youthful zest for excitement and urge for new experience was getting to be misinterpreted. I certainly had no death wish and appreciated only too well that the law of averages under the present conditions, would not permit me to go unscathed for much longer.

However, my youthful ego would not permit me to betray the image that was building up and pride coupled to idiocy would not let me back away.

"Of course sir," was my bold reply, whilst under my breath I cursed the "B company" captain for asking.

"Good man, report at eleven thirty tonight and good luck to you."

With a Mills bomb in each pocket, I reported as instructed at 11.30pm. About this patrol, I had a strange feeling. Rather like the feeling I had when Percy caught it. I hoped I didn't have to use the two bombs and that perhaps the night would pass quietly.

It did nothing to settle my insides to learn that a total of sixty men were going out in this group. That was a large patrol. The more links there are in a chain, the greater the possibility of one breaking. I preferred to be out there with a small group of experienced men. One day, I felt, I shall press my luck too far and prowling around No-Man's-Land would bring its own subtle way of telling me when I've reached my limit. It was getting to be a worry!

At midnight, we entered one of the saps to prepare for leaving. When all was ready, we filed out quietly through our own wire. With two trained scouts leading the way we began running across No-Man's-Land towards the German trench. Before long we came to a deep ravine.

The bottom of this gully was about fifty yards wide with sloping banks on either side. This was no surprise to the scouts, who had been making for it as a starting point. In single file we advanced along it, keeping very close to the left hand bank.

Progress went well until word came back down the line that a strong German patrol had been sighted, coming down the ravine ahead of us and in our direction. We stayed motionless and not a sound came from our sixty raiders. I wondered if the enemy would hear the loud beating of my heart.

We heard them come closer and closer until we could hear the sound of bayonets striking against their legs as they walked. We are in for a hell of a scrap now with no possibility of getting out of it, I thought, as we remained standing motionless.

With cool leadership, I reckoned we had the element of surprise and would capture most of them, if not all. I had not allowed for the thinking of the captain however, who obviously was not a cool leader. He had not thought it out and was prepared to risk the lives of sixty men against his deplorable lack of experience. What a pity he had taken that extra tot of rum over the allowance, before leaving our trench!

Leaving his position, which was a third of the way from the front, of our single file, and walking alongside the column, he made for the front end. He walked forward, and shouted out, in an extremely loud voice, so that all sixty men could hear him clearly

"From here - follow me." The men at the point he indicated, peeled off in order to follow him.

I joined them as one of the ten men to be led across the ravine, theoretically, in order to cut off the enemy from their own trenches.

"Does this idiot think all Germans are bloody deaf," I muttered quietly. They had now been sent a clear message of our arrival. I heard the multiple clicks, as the Germans attached bayonets to their rifle muzzles, followed by a string of orders in German.

Our officer now had, for our proposed strategy, fifty of our men lying on the ground awaiting the order to fire at the enemy. About fifty of the enemy were also lying on the ground waiting to fire at us. Fine! But our fifty had been left without a leader. The officer had left them in order to take out the ten of us, to form some sort of cut off movement.

This had now become impracticable, none functional and to no advantage. We ten were on the other side of the bloody ravine waiting to see what happened next. With only seconds to wait, the captain made another epic decision. Turning to our group of ten, he yelled **"Fix Bayonets - CHARGE!"**

We were back to hell, in that ravine. One hundred rifles were cracking and barking away in rapid fire. What a ridiculous situation, my first thought was to shed the bombs that I carried. I certainly had no wish to be caught with those on me. I knew where the German patrol was, so pulling the pins I lobbed the bombs into their midst. The other bombers followed my example and did the same. In the confines of the steep embankments the noise became deafening.

The German patrol not knowing our strength, turned back. The bombs had clinched it for us. They must have thought that we had them surrounded and they ran off up the ravine, right up past the spot where I was pressed against the wall, halfway up the bank. I gripped my rifle instinctively, but made no move.

I could have taken a few pot shots, but before I could get them all, one of them at least would certainly have retaliated. My first shot would have betrayed my position. I felt that I had killed enough men for one night, especially if they stood a good chance of taking me with them! Besides which, I had enough problems with the trouble that found me, without going out looking for it. So, that little cluster escaped and so did I.

They certainly knew where we were. The German artillery now began to scatter shrapnel shells over the ravine. Evidently any of their own men not already dead, were expendable, providing they got us as well. I had seen this sort of thing before, too!

Scrambling down the ravine bank, I came across the dead body of a German and dragged him over to whatever was left of our patrol.

"Here you are sir," I said to the captain "Here's a body." He turned to see what I had.

"Good," he answered, "Hang on to him, we can take him back with us and see if he has any useful papers, or identity for intelligence, when we finish off this crack patrol of theirs."

He intended following the patrol to their trench to finish the fight there, but the continued bombardment became much too ferocious, forcing us to retire to our own lines. We found two other German bodies to add to the first, so we carried all three back.

A surprise awaited us, when on entering our trench, we were met by a reserve battalion that had been rushed up from the rear to the front line and were standing there with bayonets fixed. It seems that those in charge thought our patrol had met a full-scale attack in No-Man's-Land and that they would be next.

Gradually, the artillery quietened down, the reserve battalion was withdrawn and the captain of "B" company thanked me for my services telling me,

"Now report back to your own company commander." Returning directly to my captain's dugout to make my report, I was greeted with,

"Come and sit down corporal, tell me in your own words everything that happened, from the second the patrol left our lines until its return to them." I gave him an accurate report, whereupon he gazed at me and nodded his head.

"I see, you were then amongst the ten men who had to carry out the bayonet charge? Where was the captain's own bombing sergeant?" I paused momentarily before committing.

"At the back sir, in case he was needed."

"In case you were knocked over you mean," he rapped. "Right, he won't use my NCOs again, that was not the arrangement, you were intended as the reserve." He thanked me for the report and handed me a stiff issue of rum, adding, "Now get back to your dugout and sleep for the remainder of the night."

Two days later the captain sent for me, saying,

"Corporal, there are a number of medal opportunities for bravery within "B" Company, or at least I am making certain recommendations. I have it in mind to recommend you. Of course if you would rather go on special leave instead, that might be arranged."

"I would much prefer to go on leave sir."

"Sensible chap! You will go as soon as we get relieved from the trenches." He was a man of his word. I had a hot bath, a change into clean underclothing, had my uniform steamed to kill the livestock and a present from the captain of twenty francs to drink his health in Birmingham.

As I had plenty of time to spare, there was one thing I needed to do before leaving. I had promised Liz that I would try to find her two brothers if an opportunity existed and a golden one was here right now. The Seaforth Highlanders in this division *were* in fact the second battalion. Not only that, but they were quite close by. I knew my chances were pretty slim, but at least I would be able to tell Liz that I had tried. Ten minutes or so was all it took to reach their position at the rest area and the first Scot I saw faced the question.

"Excuse me" I began, "I wonder if somewhere in your battalion you have two Brummies named Harry and Jim Rogers. I know it's a tall order, but I would like to find them if possible, perhaps you could tell me the best people to approach who might keep a record this side of HQ?"

I waited for him to burst into a laughing fit, or even walk away muttering some sort of Gaelic obscenity, but he did none of these things. He looked me straight in the eye, with a serious expression and said "Dya mean - Big Jim? Aye, I ken him weel, ye'll find him awar doon the track wi the Jock's Concert Party, in fact, ye cud weel say that Big Jim *is* the Jock's Concert Party and nae doot brother Hal will be there too." I was dumb struck - this was unbelievable. The first man in the area that I met knew both of them, and the whole battalion was there.

So, 'awar doon the track' I went and, with little difficulty, located Big Jim. I could see why he had been so named. I introduced myself to him and his face broke out in a broad and open grin. He advanced towards me holding out a large hand, which wrapped around mine with a warm friendly squeeze as we shook hands.

"So you're Harry Morgan," he said, "Our Liz's chap?" I soon realised that shaking hands was not the Rogers style for family, or potential family and quickly found myself in a great bear-hug.

After that he took me to meet his elder brother Harry, a more gentle and serious individual. In fact on one point we both had something in common, he was a Henry Edward that everyone called Harry or Hal, and I was George Henry that everyone called Harry. Why does no one seem to go through life with their birth-name?

We went to the makeshift hut in which the concert party performed and I was introduced to all and sundry as "Harry; our Liz's chap". Jim, like most of the rest of his family, had a good singing voice. He did some vocal, comedy sketches, stand-up comedy, writing, producing and directing. The whole thing, you name it, Jim carried the show and knew everyone as an equal.

Officers and other ranks were all the same to Big Jim and as Liz had said, "Who is going to argue with the boxing champ." Hal did some comedy and joined in the sketches, but was not so at ease with the singing, though he did some nonetheless.

The work they both put in was part time. It had to be planned between the fighting and their duties. They operated the same duty periods through the trench system as everyone else and they did their share of the fighting on the front, but found their own relaxation at the rest centre, by entertaining others.

Hal said, "Liz wrote and told us you might be in the area sometime, she also said something about the Warwick's having beaten us at football, 4-3 I think the claim was!"

"That's true," I replied "We have a good team, but the score was 4-0, you didn't play then?"

Jim was quick off the mark and with a pained expression on his face said "No, we were injured." His answer however, coincided with an equally quick response from Hal, which made the reply a duet, as Hal said, "No we were on duty." They turned to look at each other, with mock snarls of disgust.

Laughingly I replied, "Injured and yet still reporting for duty, that should deserve a medal."

"He'll get one, as soon as you have gone Harry!" Threatened Jim.

Finally I had to go and was almost reluctant to do so. I felt as soon as we met, that I had seen them both before, obviously they were in the team that we thrashed. After a parting bear-hug (brother bear from Hal, father bear from Big Jim) they started off, back down towards their quarters. I stood and watched them go. They glanced back to see me still there and with a wave Jim called,

"Enjoy your leave Harry, give our Bab a kiss from me and Hal" and they went off.

Bab, I discovered, was his pet name for Liz and also for his other sisters, as well as all children, whoever they belonged to and whatever their age. Sometimes even me. Meeting them both gave me a great deal of pleasure and would also please Liz.

When all hope of ever seeing 'home' again has been given up, to suddenly have a travel warrant thrust at you with cash and a leave pass, is such an exciting feeling as to be inexpressible. This has to be the greatest, most wonderful journey a wartime fighting soldier can make - a visit to Home.

Keep the home fires burning, while your hearts are yearning
Though the lads are far away, they dream of home
There's a silver lining through the dark clouds shining,
Turn the dark clouds inside out, till the boys come home.

Ivor Novello

Seventeen

Home Leave - *Better than a possible medal*

JUNE 1916

London did not receive me well. The town sharks were out on the prowl. Returning troops were excited at being back, and understandably, they were willing to trust everyone they met. Someone approached a group of us saying,

"Do your folks know you're on the way lads?"

"No," I replied, "No time to let them know, as we have only just got off the boat from France."

"Then how would you like me to send them a telegram from you, to tell them what time you'll arrive, you don't want to take them by surprise, now do ya? Here! I'll write down the time your train gets in and send one off for ya, it only costs two bob."

I suppose coming home lulls one into thinking that all fellow citizens are appreciative of the efforts put in on their behalf, at least if we can believe all we are told, they do. "A great idea," I said, and together with a large number of the assembled troops filling the platform, handed over the address, arrival time, short message and two shillings, to one of the many men collecting such information and offering this service.

Sadly, my arrival was not greeted at New Street station Birmingham and my family had not been informed. We had been conned. I was more disappointed in my fellow man, than I was furious at his deception.At two shillings a time, they needed only ten "mugs" each day, to provide an income of £7 per week. We were out there risking our lives and the possible destruction of family life for our wives and children, for the princely sum of one shilling each day. These bastards were doing this in perfect freedom and no one seemed to care, or to stop them from doing it openly. It gave a poor start to my homecoming.

Regrettably, I had been at home only three days when a telegram arrived for me. I did not want this. **"Return to your battalion in France immediately."** No further message, or reasons given.

"To hell with that," was my comment, but my family were most upset.

"You can't ignore an order," my father said. "And your mother will be worried about what would happen to you when you did go back afterwards."

Could they be concerned about what the neighbours would say, if they found out? I would never know, but I wouldn't worry them for the world.

I visited Liz who was also disappointed that I was leaving again so soon. It was now obvious that there existed more between the two of us than I had previously recognised. That is why going back had become more of a wrench, however, I had no choice and packed up, losing two precious days of my home leave in order to return to the rotten filth, rats and lice of France. Maybe I should have taken the medal recommendation!

There's a long,long, trail a winding, into the land of my dream
Where the nightingales are singing in a white moonbeam,
There's a long, long, night a waiting until my dreams all come true
Till the day when I'll be going down that long,long, trail with you.

Eighteen

First Battle of the SOMME
01 July to 18 November 1916

6 July 1916

My battalion, when I returned, were in exactly the same barn, in the same desolate little village, close to the Belgium/France border, where I had left them just a few days previously. Rumours were rampant, but none knew for sure. Perhaps the strangest of the rumours was that the Russians were joining the Western front and would require all sea and land transport - all nonsense of course.

Our training continued and consisted of the usual shooting and bayonet practice as well as practice for going 'over-the-top' from a trench. This obviously was for a significant purpose and reinforced yet another rumour that we were moving to the front line on the Somme. It was now 6 July 1916. Rumour became fact and fact was to become more horrific than fiction ever could be.

It was on the first day of this month (1 July) that a British main attack had been made, across an eighteen mile front from Maricourt, north of the river Somme to Gommecourt. Nineteen British divisions, of the Fourth and Third armies, hit the German Second army. The attack was preceded by a massive eight day bombardment beginning on 24 June 1916.

When this bombardment was finished on 01 July, the attack began at 7.30am. More than a half-million men advanced on that day, over No-Man's-Land. Although we often received some pieces of rumoured information, filtered down through the ranks, we could never be certain what was fact and what fiction.

Had we been told the true results of that earlier attack, before making our present one, we would certainly have felt differently about it. Much later we learned the fearful truth of that battle. That first day of July 1916, resulted in casualties of 58,000 men of which 19,000 were dead - the largest loss ever, by the British Army in one day.

So! On the sixth of July, without the advantage of prior knowledge of circumstance, purpose or intent, we started our journey to join what would later be known as 'The First Battle of the Somme.'

With alternate marches and rides in lorries, we passed through Albert and were lined up on the side of the road. We watched with admiration a battery of French .75 mm in action. What guns these were, not just unique but revolutionary. The original design was produced in 1897 and yet it became the working model for all future field guns for all armies.

Equipped with a hydro-pneumatic recoil system, to give stability when fired it also had wheel brakes and a trail spade. It stood like a rock and hardly moved when in action. The firing rate achieved 20 rounds each minute due to the rapid action breech mechanism and it sent a shrapnel shell weighing 16lb over a range of more than four miles. What a gun. I felt pleased that it was on our side!

These French gunners were certainly getting the best out of them. Stripped to the waist, faces and bodies grimed with dirt, powder and sweat. They loaded the shells almost in defiance of the insatiable hunger of the guns. A smooth continuous process, of load-fire - load-fire - load-fire. Loaders and gunners, like automatons, mesmerised by the highly trained repetition of their movements. An occasional German shell exploded near them, but they appeared to be oblivious to all, except the load-fire of the weapon.

At this same time, British troops were coming down the road escorting hundreds of German prisoners, who looked in terrible condition. Half starved, dirty, unshaven. It was impossible not to feel sorry for them. For days they had been living in hell under the terrifying bombardment of our Artillery. Their nerves were shattered, they were weak from lack of food and a starvation diet, clothing was ragged and in most cases totally inadequate for the weather conditions.

I spoke to one, who had quite good English and he assured me,

"The English forces have never been in such a bombardment as we Germans are presently going through. We have been on the receiving end of gunfire before, but never anything like this. Also, we have been without food or water in our front line for three days," he said. Hearing this, I was reminded of something I was told. Apparently a captured German officer declared at Mons that they surrendered their position because they could no longer hold out against the British machine gun fire, when in fact there were no machine guns. They had wrongly interpreted the high degree of skill displayed by a British infantry division giving "rapid fire" using short Lee Enfield rifles!

Soon, we were moved nearer to the din of battle, to be put in an old trench taken from the Germans. This was to be a short visit however, just a few hours and we were then moved out to relieve one of the regiments at the front who had completed more than their fair share of fighting. Since the war began, there have been many incidents and experiences that leave a mark. Usually the unexpected occasions are the most frightening, perhaps because there is no time to think or prepare mentally.

The battalion was once more on the move, and the march was in full flow. We carried our usual loads of about sixty pounds minimum per man, and did our best to make the required twenty miles a day without fuss. Horses and some motor vehicles pulled the heavier items, guns, ammunition wagons, supply wagons, wagons of food for the horses, and field kitchens for cooking on the march.

There were a lot of horses, some 5,000 in an infantry division when I first joined in 1914 and more than 5,000 in a cavalry division. I am not sure what the number was at this time. Vast numbers had been killed, and were replaced. There was no doubt that they were invaluable under these conditions. But they also had a tough time in the mud.

We completed our march and made camp. The old trench we had just left seemed nice while we were there. Little did I think I would wish to be back in it. A certain incident was to occur which was destined to remain with me forever. At the time, I seemed to take it in my stride, it was as if an immunity had invaded my body and placed inhibitors at all nerve centres, so that reactions had soft edges.

Nothing surprised and all happenings were there to be overcome. It was later in my life that the true horror of this particular incident was realised, when daily happenings became more normal. I used to like surprises, but not out here.

Recessional

God of our fathers, known of old,
Lord of our far-flung battle-line,
Beneath whose awful Hand we hold
Dominion over palm and pine
Lord God of Hosts, be with us yet,
Lest we forget — Lest we forget

Rudyard Kipling - 1865 - 1936

Nineteen

Field Kitchens near the SOMME - *Daytime*

12 July 1916

Our battalion had four field kitchens, which were lined up opposite us and at this particular time chimneys were smoking away as the cooks prepared dinner. We were sitting around chatting and were suddenly made aware of a familiar sound. The low toned, deep roar of a 150mm heavy German shell. "It's a coal box" went the cry, as we flung ourselves to the ground.

Everyone was prepared for this God Almighty explosion, which vibrated and trembled the earth we lay on. I raised my head to see where it had landed and met with the incredible sight of falling debris, stones, rubble, metal chunks, poles, equipment, pots, pans and almost unbelievably, human body parts.

The shell had struck directly under the field kitchens, two were upside down and two had disappeared entirely. We were all called upon to assist with the clearing up. I helped to collect some of the arms, legs, heads, hands and feet that lay scattered over the ground, whilst others dug a grave. The limbs were impossible to sort and were placed into one large grave all together. A marker cross was carved and written, bearing the names of the victims and the identity tags found were given to the Commander.

My immediate thought was 'No bloody dinner tonight then!' No sooner the thought, than yet once more, the shame. 'How about the dead? People killed and I'm worried about dinner.' It seemed however, that I wasn't the only one to think that way because someone came along and said

"We are helping ourselves to whatever supplies are laying around, there will be nothing else available tonight!"

So, that was the way it was! Right or wrong, like it or not, that was the way it was. We searched the area for boxes of army issue biscuits, now lying scattered over a wide sector. I filled my haversack, knowing that in a short time I would be going 'Over The Top' once more.

There would be many hungry hours to occupy. I sat down to eat a few, just to keep me going and could not avoid thinking about the words of Sergeant de St Croix in that No-Man's-Land shell hole. "They're your comrades, but the less you know about them the better. Don't make them your friends, you'll do them no good, or yourself either!" I think now I know for the first time, precisely what he meant. It was not the big brusque hero soldier talking. It was a man attempting to do his duty and at the same time hold on to his sanity. This perhaps, also explained my attitude to a large extent. I had shot men. I had moved their dead bodies, dragged them back to our trenches, tripped over them, rolled over them, been covered in their blood, used them for shields and shelter, collected the pieces, until it meant no more to me than it would to a butcher putting in a full day's work.

Familiarity had hardened me to such an extent that a dead body had become simply just that. I was dismissing identification and ruling out the fact of a previous "live" period for them. This, I could do, because I simply did not know them. I was now subconsciously applying what the sergeant had suggested, at the time we sheltered, back in the shell-hole.

I walked along the trench and had to pass yet another group of recently captured German prisoners. What a sad sight they made. Like the others, they were in filthy condition and half starved, certainly as bad as the previous group, if not worse.

The feeling of pity welled up once more. I reached into my haversack for a box of our hard biscuits. As I handed it down, there was a sudden rush for the contents that was incredible to behold. Never in my life have I seen such hard biscuits devoured at such an alarming rate. It was miraculous that they didn't choke.

They looked at me and spoke in German. I needed no knowledge of their language to understand how sincere was their appreciation, the look in their eyes said it all. I felt pleased to have done them a good turn even if they were the enemy, they were soldiers like me. The British officer reprimanding me for feeding the enemy could go take a running jump. He couldn't take the tin off them, it was empty, I rather carelessly, accidentally dropped another tin as I turned around to leave.

If old Jerry shells the trench never mind
If old Jerry shells the trench never mind
Though the blasted sandbags fly, you have only once to die
If old Jerry shells the trench never mind.

Twenty

Battle of Contalmaison - SOMME - *Night time*

12 July 1916

Night time: We fell-in and moved closer to the front line, our time was fast approaching. We were now in support of the front line lads who were having a rough time. As we progressed, I could see a vast number of dead, lying in the fields.

God, it was a most depressing sight. Row upon row, as far as the eye could see. Like stalks of corn, felled by the sweep of a scythe, in straight lines. It was quite plain from the position of the bodies, how it happened with those first British attacks on the Somme. The troops were ordered over in "waves" and ordered to walk, not run. They had walked into the cross fire of German machine gun posts, which let loose a non-stop enfilade of bullets - wave after wave, after wave.

In waves they walked and in waves they died. The cream of Britain's youth and manhood in their own private and perpetual silence, on this bleak night of 12 July 1916. Lives cut short, by men they never knew and had no disagreement with, for reasons they could not now be given, by the men they had never met, who had sent them out here. I began to feel sick again. Would our own leadership now accept that machine guns were a weapon to be feared, and a weapon to be taken seriously? What did they hope to gain, by walking their troops into battle, making them so vulnerable to such concentrated fire power? I trusted that their reasons were good and the sacrifice worth it![2]

---

[2] see Appendix two

Flanders Fields

In Flanders Fields the poppies blow
Between the crosses, row on row
That mark our place; and in the sky
The larks, still bravely singing, fly
Scarce heard amid the guns below.
We are the dead, short days ago
We lived, felt dawn,saw sunset glow,
Loved and were loved, and now we lie
In Flanders Fields
Take up our quarrel with the foe:
To you from failing hands we throw
The torch; be yours to hold it high
If ye break faith with us who die
We shall not sleep, though poppies grow
In Flanders Fields

John McCrae 1915

Twenty One

Prepare for Daylight Attack

13 July 1916

On the morning of Thursday 13 July, I was walking along the trench when one of the troops in my platoon called me over to him. In the mud of the trench, before him, was the body of a German, partially buried.

"Look at this Corporal" he said and pressed his foot down on the stomach of the rotting body, making a fountain of dirty water shoot upwards from the mouth of the corpse.

"Not at all funny, get away from there and leave him alone" I said as I walked away. I may be getting harder in outlook, but I hope I never go as far as that. The dead have a right to some dignity, even the enemy dead! Are we becoming desensitised to everything?

I was now able to view the area we were in by broad daylight, and the dead quite obviously numbered many thousands. What puzzled me was the fact that they had all turned black. Eyes bulging from sockets, mouths wide open, tongues hanging and also visibly black. Had they been gassed or was this the effect of the sunlight? I didn't know. They were bloated and the stench was terrible. I later learned that the blackness was caused by gas.

As I looked across the battlefield I wondered if one day soon I would be joining them. The thought was a ghastly one, to look at one single body amongst so many and think "Is that me, tomorrow?" I would soon find out. Few of these bodies would be recovered, as time passed they would sink into the mud, be shelled into obscurity, decay, or be eaten by the rats. We had just one day more here, and then we would be part of the action. Instructions were: "Tonight we move into the front line - tomorrow we attack; in daylight."

There was still time before that, for yet another little fright. At dusk I was sent out on a ration party to battalion HQ. We obtained the ration without problem and I carried two petrol tins filled with fresh water. Carelessly, I managed to lose the party on the return. I knew the way back to the battalion so it was no big deal and I entered an old communication trench.

Normally I would have walked over the top of the trench, but as we were still receiving enemy shells almost continuously, I chose the trench, found some cigarettes in my pocket and thought lighting one up would be a good idea, so the first dugout found would be the place to go. It is never a good idea to let a lightup betray your position, so a dugout in the trench was the best bet.

There was one close at hand, so I placed my two water filled petrol tins near the entrance and fumbled around the walls to find a place to sit. Once seated, I struck a match to view my surroundings and was petrified to find sitting against the opposite wall, just four feet away, bolt upright, eyes wide open and staring straight at me, the dead bodies of two British soldiers. I was transfixed, a cold shiver ran through my body, before the burning match reached my fingers and shocked me into immediate action. I was up and away in seconds.

It was a little while later that I had to go back again to collect the water. I left in such a blind hurry that I had no time to gather my senses, let alone my tins. What a damned fool I felt.

The rest of the ration party were there when I finally returned. Fortunately they didn't press me too closely for reasons of separation. Rations were distributed and we were now prepared for our tour of duty 'Up-Front'. Guides were sent along our line, to direct the different companies to their respective sectors of the front line trench and we set out.

In some way, the enemy must have known our situation and our intention, for the second we began to move they opened up a severely heavy artillery barrage. No doubt the Germans knew the length of time the present regiment had been on duty and realised that a relief was due. I am sure they knew quite a lot about our activities.

We were getting to know many of their practices, habits, systems of operation, etc. and both sides probably knew more about each other than was realised.

With heavy shells screaming overhead and the earth shaking from explosions, showers of earth, falling debris and the searing metal fragments from the overhead bursting shrapnel shells, it was only minutes before the familiar cries for **"STRETCHER BEARERS!"** could be heard from all sectors.

The wounded were carried back to our own trench whilst the rest of us continued forwards. Here we go again, I thought, this must be what they mean when they talk about 'laying your life on the line'! How many of us were wishing we could be going in the same direction as those on the stretchers, I can only guess, most certainly the thought had crossed my mind.

Eventually we reached our objective and climbed down into the trench. NCOs posted their sentries as we went through. As would be expected, the lads we were relieving lost no time getting out and who could blame them for that? They had captured the trench and with hand guns and bayonets, held it against German counter attacks. They had done their share and now it was up to us!

A sleepless night was inevitable. The ever present guns seemed to be the only things that were continuously non-stop. In fact silence of the guns would be treated with mistrust. We crouched down under the parapet, with the earth showering upon us. Our only activity for the present was to leap up and do some trench digging, each time a shell scored a direct hit, and buried a few men. As before, sometimes we saved a few.

Hush, here comes a whiz-bang, Hush here comes a whiz-bang
Now you soldier men get down those stairs
Down in your dugouts and say your prayers,
Hush here comes a whiz-bang and it's making straight for you,
and you'll see all the wonders of no-man's-land if a whiz-bang, - hits you.

Twenty Two

Attack at Dawn - *Battle of Contalmaison* - SOMME.

14 July 1916

Dawn on 14 July 1916. What would this day bring? We had in front of us the knowledge that we were to make an attack in daylight. How slowly the time went. "God, why couldn't we make the attack and get it over and done with?" The waiting, I am sure was worse than the event.

I scanned the faces of the men around me. Their expressionless stare carried a blank, faraway look, a mindless inner reflection. They were as scared as me and were trying not to show it. It was as though we had switched off in the hope that possible consequences of this day would go away.

Perhaps, also like me, they were thinking of home and family; wives; parents and children. My thoughts were with the folk I had left in Birmingham, especially Liz, my sisters, brothers and of course my best mate 1554. Will I see tomorrow's sunrise? How close am I now to finishing my life, almost before I have started to live it? Our speculations were interrupted by the sound of aeroplanes. It was obvious that their purpose was observation and they were ours. That was a relief, there were some anti-aircraft guns going hell for leather at them, but the airmen appeared to ignore it and carried on with their job.

I now looked back over the top of our trench, to see battalions of British troops coming over the fields, across the valley, in single lines towards our position, hidden from sight of the Germans their already fixed bayonets glinting in the morning sunshine. These were our Reserves who were to help us if needed. As if someone had given a signal. It all started. Our guns led the way and the German guns retaliated, first on our position then over our heads to pound the advancing reserves. They were certainly up to date with their intelligence gathering.

The cacophony of noise from screaming shells and bullets was now getting on our nerves. We could also hear the repetitive rattle of machine guns and the crack of rifle fire from the Germans holding the trench in front of us, the one we were about to take.

Our platoon officer came to us and shouted "Zero-zero, **Over-the-Top lads ... AD-VAANCE.**" We followed obediently. Over-the-top and onwards - gallantly led by this officer for a full ten yards, before he fell to the ground dead - his first and his last battle. The platoon went on in line with the rest of the battalion, but men were going down with every step forward that we took.

As soon as we came within bombing distance, we threw some of our bombs into the German trench. It made them keep their heads down for a short time and gave at least some of our lads a few more minutes of life on earth. The ground now shook from the pounding barrage, the air being alive with the ceaseless -phss- phss- phss- phss sounds of a million or more bullets with an occasional ricochet.

This was the time, the time for our first ordered charge. **"FIX— BAY-ON-ETS . . . CHARGE."** We went ahead like demons from hell, bordering on insanity, due to the combined din of battle and the inevitable fear, together with the nervous tension stored by the waiting, being suddenly given vent. We rushed ahead and down into the enemy trench.

No quarter was given, no sympathy felt. This was how it had to be. It was training come to life, but these were no longer sacks stuffed with straw on a wooden frame suspended from a rope, these were real people, like us!

A German soldier ran through the trench towards us and I was going to be the nearest one to him. He raised his rifle, which pointed in my direction and I had no choice. I fired a round from waist high, to get in first, which stopped him, then raised the rifle to my shoulder, whilst at the same time operating the bolt, then aimed and fired an accurate second round. He fell and I turned and chased after my platoon, heart racing, breathing heavily, shouting and cursing as I went.

I found a group of five who had paused to catch their breath, and joined them, still tense from my earlier experience, my chest heaving to grab more oxygen. Suddenly one of our small group yelled at the top of his voice, with a strong note of alarm, **"GET-HIM!"** An oil sheet behind me, covering a dugout, had been lifted up from the inside, and a German soldier had stepped out.

Three of us, reacting entirely from instinct and the product of endless training, lunged forward with our bayonets and all three struck home, penetrating various parts of his body. I felt sick. One man withdrew and blood spurted. The soldier screamed with pain and slid to the floor. The two bayonets remaining being pulled down with him. The second man and I both withdrew at the same time, placing a foot near the steel blades, to prevent the body lifting with our pull. If he was not dead now, he was unconscious and would die.

I turned away as another of our group shot him. Shall I ever be able to forget that dying face and the scream during his terrifying ordeal? I doubt it. I found it worse because he was about my own age! God this was awful - awful! War was not what I thought it was! It is vile.

Forward through the trench we raced looking for the enemy, our rifle magazines were emptied into them. Those not killed by the bullet died from the bayonet. No mercy! What few that were left, finally became prisoners.

Another order came along the line and was shouted to us —"ON TO THE NEXT LINE." We obviously had not finished just because we had taken one trench. So it was now over the parapet of the first German trench and onward to the next. Our artillery were now going flat out into a steady rhythm and each shell seemed to have found its mark on the trench we now headed for.

It was thanks to those Gunners and their incredible accuracy that our losses in taking the second trench, were much lighter than we had come to expect. This trench had almost collapsed and the shelling thankfully ceased just before our arrival. We were able to simply walk in. The few Germans left alive and not buried in the wall collapse, were almost pleased to see us and surrender. So far we had achieved the position, now we had to hold it.

The first duty was to post sentries and strengthen the trench walls, work in which every man had to play a part. Just as we had begun this operation a cry came from one of the sentries "THEY ARE COMING OVER." I looked over the top of the parapet and was horrified, to see thousands of German soldiers, now advancing in phased rushes. The first wave would make short spaced bounds, then fling themselves flat to the ground after about twenty yards. UP-RUN-DOWN, UP-RUN-DOWN.

The second wave behind them, would be running when the first wave were down and would run past the first wave for about twenty yards, before they in turn went down and so on, until they were close enough to us, to mount a counter attack.

We had the order "HOLD YOUR FIRE - UNTIL INSTRUCTED," but how difficult it is to resist pulling a trigger when you can see an adversary in your sights and know him to be after your blood. They were now within two hundred yards of us, and none of them got up to run forward again, they all stayed prone on the ground. What were they waiting for?

The reason for this was made perfectly clear when their artillery opened up, to give us the same gruelling treatment we had metered out to them. We were all practically buried alive by the collapsing trench walls. Then by elevating their guns, the shells were lifted over our heads in order to pound our reserves, in support. At a stroke, the bombardment stopped, which could mean but one thing. Their counter attack would now advance. **"OPEN RAPID - FIRE"** was the order. The action was then fast, furious and horrifyingly bloody.

British rifle fire and OUR Lewis machine guns, opened up from our parapet at the now fast advancing hoards of enemy soldiers running at us. I yelled the command to my bomber squad and we lobbed grenades as fast as the pins could be removed. After which we returned to our rifles for rapid fire. A total change had now taken over mind and body. I found a strangely savage delight in the sight of so many men being mown down by our guns, hundreds of men and it gave me pleasure to see it!

I was yelling and shouting with the rest **"That's for what you gave us and our mates you bastards! How do you like it! Come on - come on - come on!** We were well caught up in the insanity of the situation and our rapid fire carried with it the culmination of much hard practice. Our firing rate was at a peak. The only pause was to load further clips into our 10 rounds capacity magazines. When this terrible scene ended with their failure to take our position, the German troops turned and ran for safety.

At this point, we sent over a continued rapid fire, to hit as many as we could while the opportunity lasted. For that period of time, reality had disappeared. I seemed to be utterly lost within a developing 'will to win.' A condition that had to be achieved whatever the cost. A case of him or me! Head spinning, heart racing. Lost in a mad, mad state of near oblivion.

When it was over, we had to continue our repairs to the trench, now worsened by the enemy guns. There was no time to bury our dead; that task had to wait for darkness when we could spare the time to give them a decent burial. Many stayed with us for some while! Now was a time to calm down and return to some degree of normality, if we could still remember what that was!

tune of "What a friend we have in Jesus"

When this lousy war is over, no more soldiering for me
When I get my civvie clothes on, Oh how happy I shall be
No more church parades on Sunday, No more putting in for leave
I shall kiss the Sergeant Major, how I'll miss him, how he'll grieve.

Twenty Three

Contalmaison

14 July 1916

For my platoon, I posted three sentries, one on the firing step and the other two sitting down by his feet.

To my right, a German gun began releasing shrapnel shells overhead, so I felt it necessary to take my entrenching spade and scoop out the earth from the back of the trench, making a deep cup, or dugout, into which I could sit, well back.

I thought the two sentries seated on the opposite side were a little vulnerable where they were and I said to them both, "You are not protected from the angle of that gun where you are sitting, take a tip from me and come over on this side, dig a piece out and sit in it." They looked at each other, before one answered for both, "No thanks corporal, we are OK here, it's all going over the top." They were wrong; within a very short time, a shell came over quite low, and burst directly over our trench. I felt a painful blow to my thigh that made me choke and my head swim.

The sentry on duty, standing on the fire step, toppled head first into the bottom of the trench. The two seated below, were doubled up groaning. I called out loudly, **"STRETCHER BEARERS!"** They arrived, but sadly the two men were both dead. The sentry on duty, had been injured falling into the trench, but in addition had a particularly bad stomach wound.

The bearers placed him on the stretcher and had carried him about one hundred yards, before they met the sergeant approaching. He looked at the man they carried and knew immediately.

"Take him off there" he said, "he's finished."

I felt that my luck was still holding out - one shell to share between four of us, three dead, and me only hit in the leg. Already I was having visions of

England. The bearers turned again and came back to me. One of them took out a field knife and cut away my trouser leg, then applied a field dressing and bandaged the wound.

"Take yourself out of here corporal" said the sergeant as he walked away. My platoon officer had gone under earlier, but I thought I should report to the captain before going off. I found him further up the trench.

"Yes corporal?" he enquired

"I've been wounded sir."

"Oh my God, not another NCO, have I got any left in the company? All right Corporal, thank you for coming to see me first, be careful how you get away. Goodbye and good luck" he said.

I made my way out from the back of the trench, making full use of every shell hole, limping along the best way I could, and succeeded in reaching the low valley, out of sight of the Germans. Except for the shells, I was now reasonably safe and making for the CCS along this country lane, as fast as I could manage. Just half a mile between me and the war and already the noises were fading.

Unexpectedly, I had to leap into the ditch to avoid being run down by a team of galloping horses. It was The Royal Horse Artillery. Every man in the unit was mounted and going flat out. I can see now the image created by that team. The grim looks of determination on faces circled by chin straps, limbers and guns behind them bouncing and swaying as they swept forward.

I watched from the ditch as they reached a bank, spread out, led away the horses, prepared and positioned the guns and within minutes were in action. Shells now roaring away into the enemy lines. What a fine sight it all was, impressive, professional and spectacular. Especially now that I am out of it for a while!

These transportable field guns, had a useful advantage in their mobility, by the time the enemy spotted their position and range, they would have moved somewhere else. I got myself back to the road and carried on with my journey.

On the way, I saw a young man of about my own age sitting on the verge, as I got closer, I realised he was a German prisoner and also wounded. He was somewhat alarmed at my approach, but perhaps when he saw me limping and somewhat bloodstained, with only a part of one trouser leg, he felt a little more settled. Sitting down by his side, I asked,

"What is your name?"

He raised a hand and replied in German, obviously he did not speak English. As I had no knowledge of German at all, it became plain that we were not going to have much of a conversation. I pointed first to my leg, then to myself. He understood that and opened his jacket top to reveal a nasty shoulder and chest wound.

The mime seemed more successful than trying to speak, so I took it a stage further by pointing to myself and saying "Harry!" He nodded his head slowly, then touched his stomach and said, "Erich!" We were getting somewhere after all, by making hand signs and appropriate sounds, to convey a meaning. He scratched his name in the roadway and then wiped it out with his foot, in order to scribe a large capital H, then pointed to his wounds.

"You need a hospital?" I said, "So do I Erich!" Again pointing to my leg and then to his drawn H, then nodding my head.

"Jaa" he responded.

During these attempts to make progress, an Army Padre, who must have seen some of our concentrated efforts to communicate as he approached, stopped to say "What would I not give right now, for a camera, to take a snapshot of you two boys sitting there." There was most certainly a tear in his eyes as he took out a cigarette case, which he then offered forward, for us to take one.

Surprisingly, Erich would not light or smoke his, until he could see me smoking mine. Perhaps he thought the cigarettes had been treated or poisoned. Or perhaps he thought there was some English etiquette to be observed in regard to cigarettes received from the clergy! The Padre blessed us and went on his way. Erich and I helped each other to get up and move to the road, where we went arm in arm, helping each other to negotiate the difficulties, as we met them.

We walked along together in this way for about half a mile and were both pleased when the hospital came into view. My leg had become stiff and painful, and Erich must have been suffering considerably. On arrival, the MO looked at us both then instructed the orderly "Put them both on stretchers!" Before the stretchers arrived, I turned to Erich and took the hand of his good arm in my two hands saying,

"I know you don't understand what I am saying Erich, but good-luck mate, and I hope your wounds heal quickly!"

Erich simply said "Arry" and with a few words of German, squeezed my hand.

The stretchers arrived and we were placed on them and taken in two different directions. I hoped that Erich would be well looked after, I'm sure he would have been, but I was wishing he had been sent down the line with me. Half an hour later, I was in an ambulance being taken to a rail station. From there, a Red Cross train carried me to the base hospital at Le Havre.

The rough dirty bandage put on in the trenches, was removed from my leg by a nurse. The wound was then cleaned thoroughly before a new bandage was applied. A few days here will make a nice change, I thought, and got quite a shock when the officer came around and said

"Feel like going home for a bit?" I was dumbfounded. My wound was not particularly serious and really didn't qualify for home leave.

"You don't mean it, sir?"

"Don't I, just you watch this!" and so saying, he took my card and marked it with that lovely little Red Circle, for England.

Bombed last night and bombed the night before,
Goner get bombed tonight if we never get bombed any more
When we're bombed, we're scared as we can be
God strafe the bombing men from higher Germany
They're over us, they're over us, one shell over just the four of us
Thank your lucky stars there are some more of us
or one of us could feel it all alone

Twenty Four

Recovery at Home

18 July 1916

The next day was now a familiar process, ambulance to Le Havre docks, carried on board the hospital boat, put into a beautiful bed, wait for the vessel to move out and head for Blighty.

Once in England, I recalled the previous occasion of being wounded when the officer asked where I was from. When I said Birmingham, he sent me to Manchester. This time I was wiser, I would be ready for him. I now had experience on my side! The officer came around just as before.

"Where is your home corporal?"

"Manchester, sir!" I replied without a moment of hesitation.

He scribbled on my pad and went off. I looked at the sheet in anticipation and read, 'Cambridge Military Hospital.' "Christ Almighty you just can't win can you?" I muttered. Never mind, as long as I was home, what difference did it make what part! I loved it all.

At Cambridge hospital however, I upset the old MO early on. He appeared to be much too old for the job and a miserable old sinner. He looked at my leg and grunted,

"How is your leg?"

"All right sir, but it will be better when the shrapnel is out."

"According to your medical sheet, it has already been taken out," he snapped.

"Nobody's touched it sir, so it can't have been taken out."

His voice became harder and the tone venomous.

"I distinctly told you that it has been removed and if you answer me back I will have you taken to a prisoner's hospital and your leave will be stopped."

"Very good sir, if you insist, we will leave the shrapnel where it is, in my thigh."

The nursing sister accompanying him on his rounds, gave a little shake of her head, frowned and tightened her lips as a signal for me to shut up. I did and the matter was dropped.

After that I was dispatched to a convalescent camp at Dartford in Kent. This centre struck me as being one of the worst camps in England that wounded soldiers could be sent to. An hour of slow marching before breakfast certainly created an appetite but after that, the amount of food available was pitiful. We were always feeling on the point of starvation.

At nine o'clock we were on parade once more and split up into work parties under the control of an NCO. We then worked until twelve o'clock. At two o'clock, we went for a steady route march. At least this gave an opportunity of talking to some of the other 'inmates' while we walked along. It turned out to be a useful source of information and I learned that work was available in the town. It was Government sponsored so surely it could be trusted - couldn't it? I volunteered and found that on top of my one shilling a day army pay, I could now earn another one shilling a day, for a full day's work. Absolute daylight robbery.

The Government I am certain, would not agree to military personnel working for a civilian employer for such a low rate as one shilling a day, only the Government had that privilege. So if we were not getting the benefit, the Government must have been pocketing the difference.

The civilians must have paid the military the full wage scale and the military paid us their usual mind blowing one shilling per day, plus an additional shilling. Not only was I fighting in their bloody war, they expected me to help pay for it, in my injury recovery time!

I heard that a gentleman's large private house across the moors needed a gardener, so I applied. I had never been a gardener, or grown anything except a little taller, but what could they possibly expect for two shillings a day, Capability Brown?

At my interview, the owner told me to start work the following morning at nine o'clock. I don't think I added a great deal to the visual effect of the garden layout and in fact he must have noticed. It was a repeat of the choir master at school. Sadly, he took me off that, and I was given the less technical task of picking plums from his trees, beautiful blue black, with delicious flavour. No plums in the world taste like our plums. How did I know? Don't ask, I buried all the stones, but he did have *some* fruit for the household.

He wanted to keep me, when my task was through, but not in the garden! I was asked if I would clean the family shoes, of course I felt insulted, but being second youngest in a family of eleven, (including parents) I knew I could cope with that.

His cook was an Irish woman who seemed to be convinced that I was being starved to death from what she had heard about the camp. She was not happy unless I was eating. So, my wages may have been low, but my food intake was high. I was also missing those three parades each day at the camp. I was having a good time.

The day arrived when a visit to the doctor for inspection resulted in the inevitable A1 grade. I went off on my seven days sick leave, which as usual went all too quickly. It was good to see Liz and tell her all about my meeting with Hal and Jim. She in turn told me that the Germans were now sending Zeppelins to England to drop bombs on civilians. She saw one go over Birmingham on it's way to somewhere else. She did not know where.

I was told some time ago that two of these had raided Gt.Yarmouth in Norfolk on 19 January 1915 and two people were killed, with ten or so injured. They have been over the south quite a lot it would seem. What a despicable thing to do, involving civilians like that!

My family were also delighted to see me and I had a surprise in store. Most of the home news for parents was brought by telegram with its consequent heartbreak, but now something had happened that was so rare as to be astounding. My five brothers were also on leave at this same time. At least, their small leave periods overlapped and it meant that we had two days when we were all there together.

As you can imagine, we went out for more than just a few drinks and it was great. My father and mother were overjoyed. An announcement was made by the old boy and he declared,

"Tomorrow we all go to the photo studio on Dudley road to have a group picture taken."

"Right" said Jack, "What a good idea, what time shall we be there to meet up?" "Meet up?" said father, "Meet up? We'll do nothing of the sort, you will all arrive here, and we go from here."

"What, in a bunch?"

"No! In a squad," father replied. And he meant it. We assembled as ordered, 'fell-in' outside his little house in Peel Street and he marched us away, down Big Peel Street and along the Dudley Road. Six of us in pairs, eldest at the front. He marched at the head of the column, with mum on his arm, bursting with pride, as some of the neighbours waved us away. All the way to the studio we marched. To have gone as far into the war as this, without losing a son was unique, to have them all on

A miracle in this war, all six Morgan brothers, home in uniform at the same time, were marched to a Dudley Road Photographic Studio by Dad for a group photograph.
standing left ro right - Walter - Joe - Frank - Jack
front row left to right - Fred - Father (Arthur) - Mother - Our Harry.
Harry is seen as a Corporal, wearing his Mons Star (which would date the photograph about August or September 1916).

leave at the same time in the middle of the war, was nothing short of a miracle!

If it occurred to any of the others, I don't know, we never spoke about reasons or possibilities at that happy time. It certainly went through my mind however, that if there was a 'planning office' up there, could this be a special favour and a way of saying make the most of it lads, because shortly your luck will change?

As usual, time went so quickly and the days were far too short. After this happy interlude, it was back to the I.o.W and the same old Gradual Training Company.

Once again after just a few weeks in the I.o.W with the Lead-Swingers Guild; I wanted out. I just could not tolerate all this nonsense of men with shoulder or arm wounds, limping and hobbling on walking sticks for weeks on end. I refuse to be a scrounger and asked to be transferred to another company. The sergeant major was only too pleased to oblige and within a fortnight I was again warned for active service, this time joining a Second Line Territorial Battalion, the 2/6th R.War.R.

Twenty Five

Back to France - *Third Posting*

October 1916

This was my third visit to France and it was a quiet entrance, made without any fuss or excitement whatsoever. The third time! I was now quite a war veteran. Still only twenty-one, yet I had survived more battles than many twice my age. I considered myself lucky to have lived long enough to make three visits.

Would my luck hold out this time? Perhaps I should have made more fuss about the shrapnel that I **knew** remained in my thigh. I could have bought a walking stick and limped through the GTC with many others. I could also have demanded an x-ray. If I had done all these things, I would have gone to hospital, had the metal removed, would have missed the draft and stayed in England. But I didn't. Now I hoped that this time I would not pay the ultimate price, for my high ideals, or do I mean foolishness?

It was October 1916. No cheering crowds outside the camp this time, the people of I.o.W, like most of the British people were now tired of the war. The sight of troops going away was an all too familiar sight. They simply gazed at us with a distinct look of sorrow in their eyes and went quietly about their business.

The arrival in France was exactly the same. The French had no reason to cheer or be happy. Our arrival had almost lost its meaning. Practically every woman we saw was in mourning, wearing black as a mark of respect for a dead husband, or child.

When we reached the old base camp the one thing most noticeable to me, was that the same NCOs were all there. They were there when I made the trip for the first time, and they had been there all through the war.

Most of them knew how to bully the boys who ultimately did the fighting. Maybe that ability helped them to keep their staff jobs. A few days were spent with these 'Canaries' or Special Instructors, in their yellow coats, and I for one was most pleased when that ordeal was over, and we were able to pack and move further up the line.

The old familiar sounds could be heard as we got closer, starting with the distant crash of the guns and later the rattle of machine guns, then rifle fire. We went directly into billets, another old barn. In the morning I expected we would again be just as lousy as ever, and using all the old tricks to kill this enemy, like scratching them to death, or running lighted candles along the seams of the sheets. I hate lice!

The battalion we had been detailed to join, came out of the trenches during the night and "A" company woke us up when they came into our barn. Knowing that we were draft men, they wrongly supposed that we were all new recruits. Many of them started telling wild stories about their adventures at the front and throwing their mouths around in general.

For the time being, we simply let them get it out of their system, we could always bring them back down to earth later. For now, we helped them to drink their tea, which had been sent up by the cooks and settled down to sleep for the remainder of the night.

In the morning, the draft lined up for the CO's inspection and many of the troops turned out to have a look at we 'New Boys.' I honestly do not think that a single complaint could be made against any one of us.

Every man in that draft was a seasoned fighting soldier, experienced and highly trained. Some had been wounded four or five times and most were of the old Regular Army, or BEF. By comparison, those watching us were the new recruits.

The old colonel gave us the usual lecture from his script. Now it only raised a smile. We had heard it all before and witnessed how few of these senior officers ever saw the front. But it was all there. "Honour of Battalion - great traditions to be upheld - firm discipline - shoot you if you run," it was now all so repeatedly theatrical. We hated it, but they obviously thought it necessary.

He did, however, make some indication as to the 'New Boys' own background and the action we had seen. This came as such a total surprise to the viewing troops that they developed a higher respect for us. They made quite a fuss when it was realised the amount of service we had seen in France and they became a splendid crowd to be with.

It was my intention to have nothing more to do with bombing and to avoid tying myself in with any such operation. It was not to be! The military records in which past training courses taken had been listed, had gone on ahead of us, the battalion was already aware of our abilities. Imagine my surprise to be greeted by my new platoon officer with, "Corporal Morgan, I see you are a Bombing Instructor and Machine Gunner! Just what we need."

"I prefer the machine gun sir!" was my response.

"Later," he replied, "what we need right now are bombers."

So it looked as if I would live out in No-Man's-Land once again. I will have no choice it seems.

Call it fear if you wish, but I just felt that I had already pushed my luck to extremes and the law of averages would certainly catch up with me one day. My preference for the MG was based upon a simple fact. It is essentially defensive.

It requires only that you sit there with thousands of rounds of ammunition and wait for the enemy to run at you. You, being under cover, they, being in the open, you shoot as they approach. One MG can dispose of 500 men without much problem.

Bombing on the other hand is offensive, (in every sense of the word) for this you need to load up as many bombs as you can carry, and that is never sufficient. Creep about in the dark, (or sometimes light) seek out an enemy of unknown numbers, and get as close as you can. If you make it, you then throw all the bombs you have, which may kill those in receipt, but which also alerts many hundreds of their own kind, who come looking for you at a time when you are without defence.

At best, you can go like a bat out of hell for your own wire, your own lines, your own trench, with heavy gunfire aimed at you all the way. You can guarantee a thrashing whatever option you take. No! The machine gun will always give the best odds, and I would rather shoot at a target, than become one!

Our appointed section of the line was quiet during the first night, with scarcely a shot fired. On the second night the captain walked down the trench to advise me that a patrol was going out. He wanted me and three or four others of the draft men to go with him.

We left the saphead as a patrol, with the ordered task of looking for gaps in the German wire. The captain led us out of the sap and across some part of No-Man's-Land. We all then had to sit in various shell holes, for a period of some two hours, before he ordered us to return. You could say he had no real taste for the job! I would have loved to see his report to battalion HQ. It should have read:

Report:-

"Took six men out on patrol to spot holes in enemy wire, crawled out and hid safely out of sight in variety of well spotted shell holes for two hours. Did not see any holes in wire. Did not see any wire. Too far away don't you know! After two hours, brought self and men safely home. Did not like it much. Next patrol, respectfully suggest give the assignment to someone else!"

That's what his report should have said! I cannot help wondering what it did say! I would never know.

Back in the trench, I had plenty of thinking time once more and my conclusion was, that I was being set-up by some of these officers who were given patrol work. They had little or no personal experience, so any of them going out, requested that I be loaned to them.

I was no better off now than when I first came out here. I liked going out there, however strange that might seem, and knew the terrain so well that the danger often seemed minimal. A delusion you might well say, and you may be right, but you cannot get beyond the fact that I was still alive! Under these conditions, that must say something. It could not all be luck.

Nevertheless, I was not going to stand for being messed about any longer. If they need me that much, I must be worth more consideration than I am getting. It was a few days after this 'realisation' period when another officer requested me to accompany him on a wire inspection.

This was my chance.

"I'm sorry sir," I began, "I know how important these patrols are, and I am aware that my experience has a high value, but I am getting nothing in return. Please ask some of the sergeants to go out now and then, they get paid for it. I am on every single patrol that leaves the trench, on the lowest of pay."

Apparently stunned into silence for a second or two, he then said,

"I'm sorry corporal, we do sometimes tend to take too much for granted under these conditions and I do take your point, what is it you want?"

"For a start sir," I said, "I am not even a full corporal, only acting, yet I go out on more patrols than any other NCO in the platoon. I am, a lance corporal on lance corporal's pay, and if the captain wants that stripe back he can have it. I have soldiered out here as a private, and I can do it again."

"Well, having got that off your chest corporal, if it's stripes that you want, I agree that you have a strong entitlement and will see the captain about it. You should have promotion on the basis of bombing and machine gunning alone, not counting the work you do out here. Now, will you come with me?"

"Yes sir, I'll come with you."

He was a good man to be out there with. He went to inspect the wire and did so with a high degree of professionalism and caution. Our wire, or the German wire, the task was important to him and he did it properly. He paid me a welcome compliment by saying

"If I have to go out there again corporal, I want you with me." He was also a man of his word. Within a week I was made up to full corporal. Within two months I was made up to sergeant.

Twenty Six

Sergeant Harry Morgan

December 1916
Now, I was on a level footing with all the NCOs who had been ordering me about as they pleased, life would be a little more balanced from now on. To the privates, I was still Harry, unless there were other NCOs or officers around of course.

The front line and battle conditions in my view altered the normal strict routine of army discipline. Treat people with respect, and they in turn will develop respect for you. Certainly the colonel's threat of shooting all and sundry never worked with anyone I ever met!

Except for the occasional skirmish, no fighting worth a mention took place with this battalion for some considerable time, in fact we were enjoying life more in the front line than we did in the billet. I wondered if they had moved the Western Front to another area.

Whatever the reason, the powers that be could not tolerate this situation and we were moved on to another sector of the front, at St Quentin, where it was not so comfortable, just the opposite in fact. To look over the top of the parapet was the quickest way to leave the war - and life! The Germans were exceptional shots and their trenches were astonishingly close to ours at this point.

Having become used to the background noise of war once more, we awoke one particular morning to find everything suspiciously quiet. No sound, no movement. Some British aeroplanes came over to observe the enemy trenches and apparently had later reported that all trenches appeared to be vacated! The enemy had retired.

This business of flying over the top in a machine was a tremendous advantage and we had the benefit of the pilots view on many occasions. I for one would have hated the job, and I always held a great admiration for the chaps in the Royal Flying Corps.

There were many more of them, than when we first came here in 1914 and they now had a wireless inter-communication system with base HQ. The aircraft themselves were apparently only made out of a timber frame covered with fabric, and fitted with an engine.

They would never pay me enough to go up in one of those, yet I recall seeing a recruiting poster for the RFC showing an age requirement from 18 to 50 with a pay scale from one shilling and six pence per day to twelve shillings per day!

Still for all that they were worth their weight in gold and this was indeed exciting news to all, so we leaped out of the trench and began to walk about on the top. Orders came over for us to follow the Germans but to be careful of bombs, booby-traps, wires etc.

My own 'A' company were ordered to lead the way, which we did, slowly, into the first line that the enemy had held the previous night and hold it. 'B' company were to advance, 'to' and 'through' the first line trench held by 'A' company, advancing onward to occupy the second line trench, where they would stay and hold. 'C' company to follow through the same manoeuvre, through first and second, to third line, while 'D' company would advance through them all, to occupy the enemy fourth line.

By this means we made a steady advance, and over the period of four or five days, we had taken over a considerable area. Our scouting patrols were crawling about out there in the wilderness, not daring to make the slightest sound.

It was whilst I was out on one of these scouting parties during our fourth night of activity, that we unexpectedly came upon a man on horseback. We were totally stunned! He was challenged,

"Halt - who the hell are you?" - (our somewhat unorthodox demand.)

"One of your own bloody cavalrymen," he answered, "What the hell are you lot doing out here, crawling about playing Cowboys and Indians, you've been behind your own cavalry for four days, what a load of bloody idiots!"

This was not just a blow to our professional pride it was a cardinal error of administration and shocking leadership. Our officers knew nothing of their presence and there was a strong possibility that from a distance they might have been wrongly identified as the enemy.

Our gunners could have opened up on them to clear our forward path. Also, of course, it made the infantry look foolish in the eyes of the cavalry. No doubt they would never let us forget that incident! God forbid that my younger brother, 'Cavalry Fred' ever found out!

We advanced still more until eventually meeting a storm of bullets whistling past our ears. We had reached the German retreat point and were within their range. Efforts now had to be concentrated on digging-in with our trenches as close to theirs as we could get. A job made more difficult because they knew what we were doing and where we were doing it. We got to about four hundred yards from them and dug the fastest trench I have ever seen in my life. Spread out in single file, trenching spades in hand, each man attacked a few yards of ground.

They gave us a rough time whilst the operation lasted but within half an hour, we were under cover, in a rough trench. There would be time later to trim it out and bank it up, to provide all the comforts of 'home' that we had come to expect!

After that we would need to address the other refinements, lines of barbed wire, a sap and saphead, dugouts, latrines, and many other necessities, like the 'Traverse' change of direction bottle neck, always built into a trench in order to prevent invaders bunching and rushing down a straight line. It served to keep them in single file.

tune of "Onward Christian Soldiers"

Onward Joe Soaps Army, marching without fear
With our old Commander safely in the rear,
He boasts and snipes from morn till night, and this is very brave
But the men who really did the job, are dead and in their grave
Onward Joe Soaps Army, marching without fear
With our old Commander safely in the rear

Twenty Seven

St.Quentin -*Back to the Somme*

January 1917

In daylight the next morning, we could see quite well, the town of St. Quentin with its huge old church. There were people in the main road, but we were too far away to identify them and they were out of our firing range. I was all in favour of not firing at all, on the basis of my preference for a quite life rather than a violent death.

The Germans in the town were most likely unaware of our presence. I felt that they had made an error when the order to retire had been given and the troops in this sector, now occupied by us, had gone back too far. This was confirmed to me when a heavy attack was made just to the left of my battalion. I am sure, that it was an attempt to straighten their lines.

After a few days more, we were getting fully organised. Our people had tapped into the German telephone system and obtained information on their objectives and planned activities. It was, it seems, their intention to mount a further heavy attack and it would be in "Mass" formation. The advance information enabled us to prepare in readiness, to position artillery, bring up ammunition, all supplies, and wait.

We were not waiting for long. Thousands, literally thousands of German troops advanced as one body of men, an incredible formation like a huge living carpet moving towards us. It was like sitting on a beach watching the tide come in, but far more sinister.

Although a frightening experience, the sight of which made my nerve ends tingle with anticipation, the knowledge that the surprise would be theirs and not ours, was a great confidence booster. We received the order for **"RAPID-FIRE,"** and everything we had was thrown at them, artillery; rifles; machine guns and grenades.

Somehow it seemed to be almost a leisurely affair, perhaps because they advanced so slowly and were so tightly packed together. We could not miss. A blind man could not miss. The training we had gone through, our experience in battle to date, our musketry skills, all contributed. It transpired to be one of the heaviest single defeats so far to be received by Germany in France.

In mass formation they advanced, in mass formation they fell, most of them dead in the middle of No-Man's-Land. The British held fire when it was all over, as a final consideration, so that the Germans could come out in safety to collect their dead and wounded.

This event being achieved, a few days rest was granted before we were advised that we had served our purpose here and were due to move off to another zone.

We were now going to the place where I had experienced the heartbreaking episode of seeing all the old folk leaving their homes and possessions, the place of seemingly never ending battles, that both sides appeared to value so much, the place where I received my first wound, the front line at Ypres.

Twenty Eight

Return to YPRES

February 1917

Our final approach towards the northern sector, for the front line of Ypres after some train travel and much marching, was along a duckboard track. It was a most beautiful moonlit night and we could see quiet clearly the German aeroplane flying fairly low over us. If experience has ever been my salvation, it worked again that night. In single file over the duckboards, the captain led the way, followed closely by the sergeant major followed by Sergeant Harry Morgan leading the remainder of the company.

All of us were now in close order single file. It was the aircraft that drew my attention. He must have seen us and I puzzled over his intentions, what would he do? If he was spotting, as surely he must be, then he was in communication with someone! Who could that be?

The aircraft released two red flares directly in front of us. Almost instantaneously there were six quick pinpoint flashes of light at ground level in the distance. I had my answer. Their - ARTILLERY! – That's who!

The time we had was short. The flashes indicated that shells had been launched.

I glanced around for a deep shell hole. **"Take COVER,"** I yelled and most of the men fell flat to the ground where they had stood. I left the line and dived head first into the hole. There was the familiar roar of shells, a mighty series of explosions and flying debris covering one and all.

The first eight men in the line, including our captain, caught for the heaviest blasts. They were now dead or seriously wounded. We gathered ourselves together and sorted out dead from wounded. A party was detailed to collect them all and take them back, whilst the remainder of us carried on to the front line.

A question I frequently asked myself was where did luck end and experience begin? Out there, I think straight reckoning and anticipation played a large part in survival. Never take anything for granted. If something unusual happened there was always a good reason for it. On the other hand, maybe that's what experience is all about.

My continuous involvement had enabled me to build up a mental stockpile, an instant library of known 'best' reactions. Much of this had now, for me, become obvious. I was in some perverse way perhaps, extremely fortunate to have been involved right from the start, when things were much quieter, thus enabling me to grow with the situation.

Of course I also had the great advantage of being able to draw from the collected wisdom of the 'old regulars' and men of the BEF, who knew all that was worth knowing about self-preservation and professional caution. From their previous battles and conflicts they had a wealth of experience, which it would have been foolish to ignore.

I now looked at the action, tried to anticipate the cause, then took rapid appropriate protective measures! Much of this had become instinctive, exactly as I recalled our battalion-bombing sergeant suggesting it should be.

There were instances where I had refused to fall flat to the ground when facing machine gun fire. Now this was far from being brave or brash. It was simply that when the fire was from a trench 'set-up' where the weapon was mounted on an iron frame, the passing sentry would send over a one-pass sweep as he walked through, with another on his return.

Such fire as this would be set low, at people crawling out or laying prone. I chose to get shot in the leg, rather than risk one through the head. A sideways profile endangered one leg only, and with a bit of luck the 'sweep' would be a fast one with wider gaps between rounds, reducing still further the chance of being hit. Such bursts of fire as these seldom came back on a return swing until the sentry himself returned.

Serious direct fire of course was a different matter. Sent over normally at body height, falling to the ground in such an instance would be preferable. I now trusted my own experience and so far it had seen me through. Long may it continue to do so!

Another officer replaced our captain and we gave the duckboards, a wide margin. These duckboards were now too well known as a target and had become a danger spot. Several times during our journey, the Germans sent over a salvo of shells, aimed on the duck-boards, they obviously had the range calculated accurately, but, because we were no longer using them, the shells were now well off their mark. Luckily for us!

My platoon was finally dumped into an outpost consisting of one dugout with just a few yards of trench either side of it. I felt that I needed some knowledge of the layout in front of us and climbed up to the top of the trench. Perhaps it would be possible to see exactly where the enemy were and how far away.

Once again the Germans proved their awareness and thought me too inquisitive. I obtained the information I wanted, but also something additional that I could well have managed without. A shell screamed over and burst directly in front of our tiny post. Ducking down, I slipped. There was a sudden severe pressure as something hit me across the ribs and in the next second, I was flat on my back at the bottom of the trench.

Struggling to get on my feet, it was plain that my ankle had been badly sprained. One of the lads helped me get to my dugout, where I could assess the damage. My tunic, cardigan and shirt had been shredded. I also had a new wound in the side of my body, below the ribs, about four inches long. My third wound, but this time getting to hospital would not be easy. With my ankle in its present condition, walking was not possible.

A stretcher-bearer assisted me as far as battalion HQ and there I had to await the arrival of the ration transport. Three or four hours went by before it appeared. Rations were then unloaded and I was placed into one of the limbers. The driver was keen to be away from there at full speed. I didn't blame him for wanting to get out of the danger zone quickly, but for me, the journey to the field hospital was hell.

It made the experience no easier to bear, when I recalled the first ambulance ride I had to take in 1914 also from the front line in Ypres. At that time I lay on my stretcher 'willing' the driver to go faster, knowing that a fellow passenger had a bad stomach wound! God has a strange way of teaching his lessons!

Anthem for Doomed Youth

What passing-bells for these who die as cattle?
Only the monstrous anger of the guns.
Only the stuttering rifles' rapid rattle
Can patter out their hasty orisons.
No mockeries for them from prayers or bells,
Nor any voice of mourning save the choirs—
The shrill, demented choirs of wailing shells;
And bugles calling for them from sad shires.

Wilfred Owen - 1893 - 1918

Twenty Nine

Out of Field Hospital - *back to Ypres*

April 1917

Three weeks in hospital and afterwards, back with my platoon in A1 condition. They had been at rest for a few days and as I joined them they were preparing to return to the front line.

That period of rest now over, the men 'filled me in' so to speak, with their rest activities, which it seems had consisted of sham battles, bayonet fighting, and bombing practice. It was great fun sergeant, what a pity you missed it! they said.

In fact they had been worked unusually hard in the period and although starved of information, they all realised that it was for some as yet unknown purpose. Meeting up later with some of my fellow sergeants, I hoped to find out what was really happening.

"What good timing Harry," one of them joked. "Back just in time for a scrap, something's coming off when we go up the line next time, but nobody is saying what."

"Is anybody saying when?" I asked.

"You've got to be joking, since when did we qualify to know what goes on? The Germans know more than we do!" This brought laughter and agreement all round.

They were right of course. We seemed to be treated like school children. Perhaps they thought if we knew what was happening, we might take our bat and ball and go home. If the top brass expected us to fight and die on their behalf, in order that they could obtain historical credit for any success we might achieve, then surely we had a right to know when, why and how!

My platoon officer, 2nd Lt.Sowerby, belatedly came to me with the same slip of paper that he had now given to all NCOs. It was entitled 'What a

Platoon Carries in Action.' I still have that same slip of paper in my possession today, signed by him. He was, in my opinion, the most gallant officer ever to take men into action. We moved away from billets one night, well aware that 'something' was going to happen soon.

Lt. Sowerby led us to an outpost and made a statement in quite a casual manner, which I thought was unusual and a strange thing to say.

"Here we are men! You are quite safe in this place, nobody has ever been over-the-top from here!"

Half an hour later a battalion runner came up and spoke to him closely. The officer called me to him. "Take charge sergeant until I get back, I have to go to battalion H.Q." I looked at my watch to see that it was then eight o'clock. The lieutenant returned at 09.30pm. "Gather round me, all NCOs, I want to talk to you," he called.

Clustered around him we listened carefully to what he had to say. "At ten o'clock sharp, which is zero, our guns will give the German lines a fierce bombardment and I do mean fierce. At 10.10pm precisely 'C' company will go over-the-top from our left, together with," his eyes met mine as I finished the sentence for him and said "Number one platoon of 'A' company, sir."

"Correct, sergeant, number one platoon of 'A' company. For how long have you known that?"

"From the moment you commented that no-one has ever gone over-the-top from this trench sir," he let it ride without further comment and continued

"So! There we are then, number one platoon of 'A' company will go over WITH 'C' company, but exactly one minute BEFORE them.

By this means, 'A' company will draw the enemy fire, to enable 'C' company to make an attack from the left and capture the position. In other words, gentlemen of 'A' platoon, it would appear that we are a sacrificial lamb and we are expendable: BUT, for Gods sake do not express that comment to the men!"

I was certainly dumbfounded. How simple it was for some distant general to instruct that one platoon could be sacrificed in order to make life for others a little easier to manage.

And how easy for our CO to select from his battalion's sixteen platoons, just one, that he knew he could rely on, yet could manage without, if he had to. All decisions from HQ of course, way back. As his choice included me, was this to be my time? Did this spell out the end of my incredible run?

Far away from Wipers I long to be
where German snipers can't get at me
Damp is my dugout, cold are my feet
waiting for whiz-bangs to send me to sleep.

Thirty

'C' Company Fails

May 1917

At exactly ten o'clock, the bombardment began. Our artillery threw everything they had at the German trench and the Germans retaliated with their own artillery, blasting our trench almost inside out.

"Don't they know *we* are supposed to be making this attack sir," I shouted out to Lt.Sowerby.

"You'll soon see whose attack it is when our barrage lifts," he answered. Most of us lit cigarettes while we waited. It could be the last one for many, or all of us. The barrage suddenly lifted, to give a changed trajectory to the shells, sending them higher and longer, to smash into the German support trenches behind their front line.

Our officer clambered to the top of the parapet and stood there for a few seconds, viewing the scene.

"Come on number one platoon, let's get going," was his cry, and every man climbed to the top and followed him towards the objective. It was as lively a time as I have ever known, shells screaming overhead and bullets from both sides British and German, whistling and hissing past us in their thousands.

From observation, it was quite obvious without too much concentrated study, that at least half of our platoon had already been lost. Being next to Lt.Sowerby, I turned my head to shout to him, but had time only to open my mouth, before seeing a bullet hole appear in the centre of his forehead, bubbling out a stream of blood that ran down his face.

He slumped to one knee, yet still managed to raise the bolt knob of his rifle that he preferred to carry in addition to his pistol, draw back the bolt and eject the cartridge case, then close the bolt and fire another round for a last shot at the enemy.

156

He died in the process. Died making the attempt, and I remember him as one of the bravest and best officers with whom I ever served. He was a lion among fighting men and a thorough gentleman. However, just like us, he was expendable.

Going forward, we threw ourselves to the ground about twenty yards from the German trench. We opened up a rapid fire, but without effect. It was a totally hopeless situation. In the darkness we had no target at which to aim. A machine gun was cutting the ground in front of us to shreds, whilst from the trenches we were receiving thrown bombs. We had no chance at all like this.

Officer now gone, I was the most senior NCO remaining, which meant I was now officially second in command of the platoon. I looked around for the supposed 'one minute later 'C' company, expecting to see their attack, but could hear or see nothing.

Not a soul in sight to the rear, or either side of us. It was painfully obvious that something had gone drastically wrong and that we could now do nothing out here without support and heavier weapons.

I shouted for what was left of the platoon to retire to their own trench, meaning for them to do it the way they had been trained. Instead, two men leaped to their feet, turned around and ran hell for leather.

Luckily for them, they got away with it and made it back in a hail of wild bullets, some of which could have struck others less fortunate, sheltering out there. So close to the enemy, attracting unnecessary attention, it was a senseless thing to do.

I began, like the remainder of the others, to crawl backwards, keeping close watch on the German trench, back, back, and further back, until at last my feet located a shell hole into which I could slide. With all the activity going on above, I concluded that I would be safer here for a while. With this consistent gunfire, crawling about up there was no place to be. I even risked a cigarette as the hole was quite deep, and smoked it whilst crouching on the bottom. After a short time, I had a compelling urge to turn around and look up. I didn't at first give in to it, but the feeling grew stronger, and I felt now, that I should.

I gripped my rifle more tightly, slipped my finger to the trigger and released the safety catch with my thumb. I turned around and looked up. I am sure that had my chinstrap not been in use, my helmet would have lifted into the air.

Kneeling on the top edge of the hole, and staring down at me, was a soldier. Sweat poured down my cheeks and down my back, 'Shall I shoot him?' 'Why had he not shot me?' I didn't know what to do, my only response was to stare back at him, and in that position we both seemed to freeze!

We must have been like that for what seemed to be at least five minutes before my common sense took over, and I started looking at what I could see, instead of what I *thought* I could see.

There was the open mouth, the awkward and uncomfortable way he was kneeling. In that pose, he could never remain motionless for any length of time. The shooting had stopped, and the abrupt silence made the situation far more eerie.

The more I studied him the more my confidence recovered. It was time for me to climb out of the crater, without losing sight of him. He remained still and his head did not turn to follow my movement, so I crept around the hole and went towards him. Making contact now, confirmed the inevitable, he was dead.

Obviously, he was from a Scottish regiment, but nothing indicated which one, and there was no additional identification. Had I understood more about the tartan, no doubt that would have provided the answer. Unwilling to leave him like that, I slung my rifle on my back and dragged him over the edge of the hole, and down to the bottom of it. At least he was now under cover, and I felt satisfied to have done some small thing for him. All that remained now was to get back to my own trench, but which way was that?

Out in No-Man's-Land, the place that some time ago was almost a second home to me, now I hadn't a clue which way to go. A star shell went up. Must be one of ours I thought, so I go that way. I made for it and recognised a German outpost, so turned and went in another direction. Getting within two yards of an old disused trench, I could hear the familiar sshw, sshw, sshw, zipping past my head.

Bullets! I had been spotted again! No time to hesitate, a two yard fast dash and into the trench. With one great energetic leap, I was in the trench; up to my chest in the most evil smelling water you could ever imagine. Trench water which as usual, was fouled up. The same old lack of drainage, coupled with the sanitary and daily waste of thousands of men, rotting corpses and the rest of it. Many trenches now contained two or three feet of water, whilst many others were completely unusable just like this one. Being impossible to dig out, or drain, they had been abandoned.

That was it, the end, the finish! "Harry," I said out loud, "If you die like this, you're a bloody idiot. Get out and walk over the top. Better to get shot and have done with it than sod about in this manner. Get out and stay upright, if they strafe the ground with machine gun fire, you'll get it in the leg, if not, you won't be much worse off than you are now!"

So I scrambled out, fed up to the teeth, tired, soaked to the skin, smelling like God knows what and cursing everything and everybody as I walked furiously in my newly chosen direction. The correct one, as it happened, but at the time I wasn't certain and somehow it just didn't seem to matter. If the whole German army had been brought out just to shoot at me, in my present state of mind, it would have been no surprise at all!

I came across another trench of unknown ownership, but who ever it belonged to, I had no intention of jumping into it. A leap over the top seemed a good idea however. Poised for the takeoff, I was just ready to jump when a low voice called,

"Who are you?"- If nothing else I was startled, my balance once lost could not be regained and my weight distribution was on the wrong foot.
So much so, that I lost my grip and slid down into the trench, only to have a bayonet thrust roughly at my throat. The same voice repeated,

"Shan't ask you again, who the hell are you; tell me or I shoot?"

"**SHOOT**; you daft bastard." I snapped.

There was a pause, an uneasy silence and then;

"Bloody Hell," the voice said, un-believingly, "Harry! It's you. I nearly stuck you with me bayonet."

"Thanks for changing your mind" I growled, now recognising the sentry.

"Where the hell have you been? Christ, you're soaked and smell like a pig farm."

"I'll tell you some other time," I said, walking away from him to find my own trench.

After what passed here for a 'clean up,' some old clothes were found and at least they were dry, the best that could be arranged in a trench. I then went to find some of the other lads. It seems that the two men who stood and ran for cover were also lucky, they made it back some hours before me. Getting together later with a water bottle full of rum, we held a small celebration of our own. When it was revealed to us that we were the only three survivors, out of all thirty sacrificial lambs, we felt that that a celebration had been well and truly earned. We drank our rum and lived happily ever after, at least for the rest of that night.

I imagined HQ would want some sort of report and set about preparing one. They did, and I had it ready for the runner when he arrived to collect it. Runners were still our only means of communication. This was certainly no terrain for bicycles.

We were sent yet another new officer to take over our post, who would not have lasted ten minutes with the late Lt.Sowerby. I hated him the second he set foot inside my trench. He selected what he thought to be the safest place to sit then called out to me:

"Sergeant"

"Yes, sir?"

"Will you please see that a stretcher is placed across the top of the trench over my head. It may possibly rain tonight."

"Yes, sir," I had the stretcher placed, as instructed. An hour later, it was:

"Sergeant."

"Yes, sir?"

"Will you please have an oil-sheet placed over the stretcher to hang down each side, to just off the floor."

"Yes, sir," I had the sheet placed, as instructed. When in place, he could not be seen at all, by anyone! An aircraft came over and the oil sheet was pushed from the inside away from the trench wall and the officer's head poked out. He looked startled,

"Is it one of ours sergeant?"

I gathered his fear would be of the enemy, so, although I knew it to be a Sopwith, I disturbed his peace of mind a little further by assuring him it was German.

"Oh dear" he said, "Keep perfectly still, tell the men not to move, don't show a moving target." Having given its order, the head was quickly withdrawn, to the illusion of comparative safety within its cover.

"Yes, sir."

I walked up the line saying as I went along, "Don't move men, enemy aircraft above, stay still, don't let the aircraft see a moving target."

The troops huddled in their dugouts couldn't understand it at first.

"What's up sergeant, it's one of ours you know it is! It's one of them Sopwith's."

"No it isn't," I replied with a wink, "It just looks like a Sopwith." I then went back to report to the officer, but for the rest of that day, he refused to leave his stretcher hide out.

It didn't take the men long to realise his limitations, or to produce some lifelike impersonations (further up the trench). He should have been found a desk job somewhere, or sent home. He was worse than useless, he was a danger to us all. He continuously asked "Whose is it sergeant?" Every time he heard an aircraft, and each time I informed him "German sir," at which, he would make the same request in the same way, "Oh dear! Keep perfectly still everyone, perfectly still, perfectly still, tell the men sergeant, tell them to keep perfectly still!"

We were relieved that night by another battalion and were more than pleased to get away. He was to lead us out and came out of his stretcher cover for the first time, in order to do so. We were out of the danger zone in record time. What a brilliant sprinter he proved to be. It was extremely difficult to keep up with him, but we managed it! A remark from one of the lads summed it up well, panting to regain his breath after the effort to keep up, he gasped "Blimey, I think his last regiment must ave bin the thirty first Fleet of Foot."

The night was spent in concrete 'Pillboxes' small, heavily reinforced gun emplacements, with firing slits, captured from the Germans. In fact the German accommodation that we captured, was nearly always found to be better made and far more comfortable than ours.

Their trenches were deeper and now this year many of them have concrete sections. I think the British policy was 'If you make it too cosy the men will not want to leave it, keep it rough cold and wet and they will be pleased to get out.'

After that, we went further back to a tented area and were squeezed, sixteen men to each Bell Tent. The battalion was ordered to turn out 'On Parade' and for the first time I can ever recall, we were told why the recent attack failed.

Naturally it was the fault of the men otherwise, it would have been hushed up. The colonel's own words probably explain it best.

"I want you all to know this," he said: "Number one platoon 'A' company, were ordered forward and they obeyed this order, to a man. The first wave of 'C' company went out as ordered, to a point some twenty yards from their own trench. At this point, they were ordered to lay down, with rifles loaded and bayonets fixed, facing the enemy lines. This, they did. The second wave of 'C' company were ordered to go out, past the first wave, and lay in front of them by about twenty yards, in the same manner.

They did not obey that order! The second wave went out as far as the first wave and stopped at that point, to lye on the same firing line as the first wave! And so, I regret to say, did the third wave, which should have spearheaded the attack, with the first and second waves immediately following. In this useless block, the three waves of 'C' company all stayed, with total disregard to the orders given.

That was as far as any of them got and the attack was never attempted. In consequence of this, number one platoon 'A' company, which had gone out one minute before, had drawn all enemy fire and were left out on their own without sufficient support or adequate firepower, ammunition or resources. Number one platoon 'A' company was practically annihilated. That was the reason for such a miserable failure.

It must be said, that if 'C' company had carried out their orders and done their duty half as well as number one platoon 'A' company, we would undoubtedly have taken the position. Mark my words well 'C' company I will **make** you take it yet!

Fortunately for 'C' company, he did not have the opportunity to carry out his threat. After a few days under canvas, we were all moved to a quieter part of the war, away from Ypres. I have often thought how strange and unusual this was. They were not usually so benevolent or considerate. Why move everyone out? Was someone in 'C' company, sufficiently precious to someone else, who knew someone able to pull a string or two? Some of the officers had well known backgrounds!

Cynical perhaps, but we were moved to a quiet spot for no identifiable purpose and moving so many men at the same time, would have been an excellent act of identity concealment, for one or two individuals later to be moved out.

Brother Bertie went away, to do his bit the other day
With a smile on his lips and his Lieutenant pips upon his shoulder bright and gay
As the train moved out he said, remember me to all the birds!
Then he wagged his paw and went away to war
shouting out these pathetic words,
Good-bye-ee, good-bye-ee, wipe the tear baby dear from your eye-ee
Though it's hard to part I know, I'll be tickled to death to go
Don't cry-ee, don't sigh-ee, there's a silver lining on the sky-ee
Bonsoir old thing, cheerio, chin chin, narpoo, toodle-oo, goodbye-ee

Thirty One

A Man of Wire

June 1917

Our newly entered quiet part of the war, turned out to be only temporary. I had always felt, that if my guess had been correct about an extraction of certain personnel, the next move would be to get the rest of us back into action. Time enough had gone by, to remove any valuable elements of 'C' company, without drawing attention, therefore it was no great surprise to me, that orders were issued and we were back in action.

We were to worry and unnerve the enemy at all times, by continuously raiding them. My battalion was fortunate in regard to these raids, for on our right we had a cavalry company in the trenches, doing the work of infantrymen. Why that was, I never really knew. Perhaps our increasingly heavy loss, of men and horses to German machine guns, plus the unsuitability of this terrain for horses, is getting through to someone.

Many of our generals have a cavalry background. Perhaps the sight of thousands of dead horses, over all the battlefields of France and Belgium is making a strong point. It must surely indicate that horses for attack, are no longer the most efficient way to win a battle, in this age of machine guns, aeroplanes and tanks?

The cavalry men did their infantry work well. Bombing raids took place almost every night. In fact they made so many, that our efforts were not required and we were not called upon to join in.

Another officer had been posted to us, who had a fetish about barbed wire. He loved it! Using so much, that one of the lads suggested his father must own the factory making it.

He had no regard for quantity and insisted on more placement, even if the area was choked with it.

"Sergeant" he called, "I'm having six rolls of wire sent up, so select a few men and supervise to make sure it goes out tonight."

"Yes sir."

I went out on my own first of all, to see where it was needed. It was quite plain to anyone who took the trouble to look, that the battalion we had just relieved had already attended to it. All new wire, just fixed, no gaps, a really super job. There was simply no space at all, anywhere for more wire. However, I had been given an order, and an order had to be obeyed; and so it would be, I had my methods!

"You six men come with me." Having selected the men, we went out that night with six rolls of shiny new barbed wire.

"Christ; Harry, where are we going to put this lot, over by the German trenches to help them out a bit?" they asked.

"No! I already know the place, just a little further on." We arrived at a shell hole, "Now, sling them all in there," I ordered. With their entrenching tools, which they had been told to bring, and to their delight and amusement, the rolls of wire were quickly covered over with soft soil, taken from the sides of the shell hole. When finally buried out of sight, we sat around chatting and smoking for an hour or so, before returning to the trench.

The officer visited our post again during the next morning.

"The wire is out, sir," I reported. "And I would like to request that you come with me to inspect it."

"Is that really necessary, sergeant?" he said, I could tell he was not too keen on the idea.

"I think so, sir, just in case of doubt later on, if we are accused of not attending to it sir."

"Yes! Of course, you are perfectly correct sergeant. Let's go."

He followed me, to inspect the new wire that we hadn't put up.

"What a fine job this is, sergeant. It's a grand piece of work you have made a fine job of it. Let's get back to the trench again now please, I have a lot to do."

We entered the trench and as casually as I could, I said to him,

"If you don't mind sir, I really would appreciate it, if you would spare the time in your busy schedule, to say a word or two to the men who did the job, just to give a little encouragement for the efforts they made."

"Certainly sergeant, of course I will." And he did, finishing with the words

"You have done a fine job out there, in poor conditions, under stress. It is a most sound and solid defence barrier, and you can be proud of it. You have all done a good nights work. Thank you!" The men loved it!

If you get stuck on the wire, never mind
If you get stuck on the wire, never mind
Though the lights as broad as day,
when you die they stop your pay
If you get stuck on the wire, never mind.

Thirty Two

Briefly at Cambrai — *Heroes are where you find them*

July 1917

The battle of Cambrai was our next calling point. However, by now one battle had become much like another. We had the usual problems of getting up supplies, food, and water. What we brought back was difficult to store. Fresh water was now a major problem.

We were hungry, thirsty and lousy most of the time. We saw our pals go down, we picked them up, dug them out, or we buried them. One event I recall, concerned a battalion of British Guards who made a splendid attack, in which two lines of German trenches were captured. We were given the order to relieve them and hold the ground taken.

We took possession and within a few hours we fell victim to an atrocious German bombardment. - **"STAND TO"**; was the order. We knew this meant a full scale counter attack and crouched under the parapet waiting for it to come. About fifty or so yards away from me, was an elderly regular I used to tease about his huge moustache, sergeant Ted Hopkins, another good mate.

"Keep well down Harry lad," he shouted.

"Any lower than this, I shall come out in Australia Ted" I called back.

At this point a crowd of our troops came rushing along the trench past me, some of them frantically claiming that we were surrounded. At the same time the severe barrage stopped and I raised myself, to look over the top. Usually there was a good reason for the stopping of guns and this was no exception.

Hundreds of Germans were advancing towards us quite quickly. Something obviously needed to be done to stop our own 'evacuating' men from going off, even if only for as long as it took to slow the advancing enemy down. At their present speed of advance, they would be upon us before we left the trench.

"Stop all those men from moving down the trench Ted," I yelled to him at the other end, "Get them on the step and make them open fire, or else none of us will get out."

He turned inwards towards me and yelled **"STOP."** We both now faced each other on the fire step and the men were between the two of us on the floor of the trench. I felt that I had no alternative but to scream at them.

"If you don't get on this bloody fire step and start shooting the enemy, I shall shoot all of you myself!"

The old colonels' would have been proud of me. It was neither bluff nor bravery on my part, just common sense. If they ran, we would have been unable to stem the tide, and would have been swept away in no time at all. It was simply self-preservation.

From the other end of the trench, the voice of Ted, also pointing his rifle at them, came through strongly,

"And any he might miss, I shall bloody shoot," he shouted. They came to their senses quickly and obeyed. We all put up a game attempt but our numbers were still too low. The enemy went down in heaps, but we were losing the fight and had to retire, though without doubt we had slowed down the enemy advance considerably.

It appears that the company on our right had broken ground letting the enemy through and we *were* almost surrounded. Not knowing that at the time, we would have stayed with it and been wiped out. Only the cry of a young officer running past us shouting "Get Out- Get Out - RETIRE, FOR YOUR LIVES" saved us from certain death. We followed him and most of us escaped safely.

We had unfortunately lost every inch of the ground taken by the Guards, but could not avoid it, we had done our best. The Guards were brought back in to join with our battalion and together we made what was recorded by some, as one of the most compelling and brilliant bayonet charges seen in France. We finally repossessed all the lost ground and this time held it.

After being relieved we moved back to the rest area where the whole brigade was ordered to turn out on parade. Formed in a square, we had no idea what was about to take place. I did notice that about twenty officers, NCOs and men were lined up in the middle of the square. Ted Hopkins being one of them.

The brigadier general was driven up in his staff car and began to relate the brave deeds of the assembled men, before pinning a medal on each one. Reaching Ted, he read out his regimental number and continued:

"Sergeant Hopkins has been recommended for, and been granted, the

DCM for gallantry in the face of the enemy. He collected stragglers and opened a heavy fire on the enemy, inflicting severe casualties and slowing down the enemy's advance."

He then pinned the medal on Ted. Dear old chap, in truth, he would not have moved if he hadn't been prompted with an instruction from me and he only threatened the men, to give some back-up support to my command. He then did what we all did, and left when we all left. Ultimately, everyone took the logical action necessary to try and save ourselves, even the men whose initial panic caused them to run. Not to worry! He was a good pal, good luck to him. Ted's only regret was that I was not included. I suppose that would have been nice. It would have shown some sort of appreciation.

Old soldiers never die, never die, never die,
Old soldiers never die, they only fade away.

Thirty Three

Briefly at Arras

August 1917

After Cambrai we were sent to Arras, but took no part at all in any fighting. So far as my record of wartime experience is concerned, no mention need be made of that. It was remarkable how the whole landscape and environment of France had now changed, even to the casual observer.

In 1914 when shells were sent crashing and bullets were flying, the birds rose out the trees in alarm, flocks of them would take wing in panic. During the following silences the birds returned to their nests in the trees. No birds could be heard now, and the once green trees in the fields and woodlands, had been transformed into a devils cauldron of blackened stumps. No branches, just black, stark, gnarled, charred, stumps. The trees were as dead as the bodies of horses and men to be found surrounding them. Here and everywhere we went. Was death following us, or were we following death?

In this area on 9 April 1917 (just four months ago) a massive five day artillery bombardment was begun by the British force. Some 2,800 guns were used on a 14 mile front. Six divisions of the German Sixth Army, against the 14 divisions of the British First Army and Third Army.

The Canadian Corps of the First Army took a section of Vimy Ridge after three hours of continuous heavy fighting. In order to take attention away from his intended offensive at Ypres, Haig renewed the attack on Arras once more on 3 May. Apart from the small gain of Fresnoy - it failed, but continued through May, though much scaled down. At the end of the whole period:-

British losses were - 150,000 men - German losses - 100,000 or more

And we gained six miles of the Hindenburg Line

tune of:- **"Boys of the old brigade"**

Send for the Boys or the Girls Brigade,
to set old England free,
send for me Brother, me Sister or me Mother
but for Gods sake don't send me.

Thirty Four

Back to St.Quentin *-The Courts Martial*

September 1917

From Arras, we returned again to St.Quentin where it was my delight to see what has to be the finest dugout ever built. It was a marvel. Built by German troops before they retired, large enough to hold every man in my battalion.

Down eighteen steps and into a vast corridor, which ran under the full length of a railway siding. Off this were scores of rooms branching off on either side, after the fashion of a large hotel. Every room had electric lighting from a huge generator, which was at the far end. It could be heard plainly, buzzing away all the time. No question of a sergeant major yelling **"Light's out,"** he would simply throw the switch.

The first night, in what to us seemed like an underground palace, was quite exciting after living like moles for so long a time. The following morning, we were warned for a later working party up at the front line.

We left at eight o'clock pm in the pouring rain, reaching the firing line within half an hour. We worked (and rested when possible) until two o'clock the following morning, then marched back again to our palace. By this time, I was tired, wet, muddy, worn out and fed up with everything.

An officer with a note pad, entered to enquire:

"Any NCO's here wish to apply for a commission?"

"Yes sir, put me down for it." I had lost count of the times I had applied, but determination costs nothing but time, why not try again.

I was beginning to think that a better education would have given me a stronger opportunity, but now they were losing so many officers perhaps the choice was narrowing, and maybe experience would count for something.

Time was beginning to drag. The weeks went by, and so did the months. I celebrated my twenty second birthday out here on November 21st, but I

172

think the achievement of still being alive was a greater celebration. Sadly our duties had now become mundane, simply to relieve the front line, do our six days, then be relieved and back to the palace, with all its comforts and modern lighting.

So much time had passed since I made my application for a commission, that now we were into late December, I had almost forgotten it. Surprised, I most certainly was, to be warned by battalion HQ to proceed to brigade HQ for an interview with the brigadier general. On arrival, I found him to be a most likeable man to talk to. He made me feel at ease, throughout the whole period of interview.

This was an important event for me and I felt that as an officer, I would be expected to hold an opinion and be able to express it. A good impression therefore had to be made, so 'be bold' was my decision.

He asked several questions about where I had been and what I had done, but it was getting rather sketchy. I ventured to say

"Sir, if you will permit me, I think I can give you a broad outline of my record in France more directly."

"Very well" he agreed, "Go ahead!"

So, still standing to attention, I went through a potted history of my service from the Isle of Wight draft, indicating dates and places of battles, wounds and recoveries, before finishing with my present platoon.

I think he was genuinely surprised, judging from his comment, "A splendid record sergeant, I promise you, I will do everything in my power to see that your application goes through. I must however, mention just one thing. You may or may not be aware that a second lieutenant's pay is not large. In some cases of emergency you may have to be prepared to put your hand in your own pocket, to help yourself out?"

"Certainly sir, I understand that," I said.

It must be confessed however, that I had no idea at all what he was referring to and presumed it to be mess bills or other costs of that sort. Whatever he meant didn't propose any fear for me, as I felt that if I could manage on my present pay, an officer would have to get more than that. Pay was the least of my concerns.

"Very well then, you will most probably hear more about this in the near future."

I decided a little drink would not be a bad idea, not a celebration of course, just a little drink of appreciation for at least making the first tiny step. I went into an Estaminet and found there another 'Warwick." Not the same battalion, if I remember correctly he was with the 15th. He looked depressed, so I asked if he would like a drink, he hesitated then looked rather puzzled, as if in some sort of shock. After half an hour or so, I not only knew why this was, but felt so badly that I just could not get it out of my mind. Even to this day recalling our conversation I could weep.

It seems he was a part of one of the Ypres attacks, close to Paschendaele. His 'A' Company men were moving out to the front line over a single duck board track, which covered a narrow strip of firmish land, over the sea of mud. I was only too well aware of this glutinous mire of foul smelling ooze, so I could visualise his description.

A soldier had been across earlier and had stumbled, or for some reason stepped off the duckboard and couldn't get back. Now he was bogged in to above knee height. He pleaded for help and the officer instructed four of the men to do what they could, but not to take too much time before catching up with the company.

They tried pulling him in with their rifles and even tried to get the rifles under his armpits. They could not get the leverage, could not apply sufficient pressure, and could not step off the duckboards. He was just that extra few feet out to defy everything they were able to try.

Eventually, they had to give up and told him others would no doubt pass and perhaps be better equipped. They then made off to catch up with the main group. Duty demanded it. They spent the next two days in the front line.

On their return journey over the same duckboards, they were horror struck to find the poor chap still there, but now only his head was visible. He was rambling, burbling, shouting and crying. Eyes opening and closing continuously, he was now stark raving mad. The troops passed by, feeling sick to their souls but by now there was nothing anyone could do. It would have been a mercy to have shot him. My companion did not know if anyone had! What a ghastly incident!

Returning back to my battalion, my 'DCM' pal Ted Hopkins was the first one to greet me with

"How did you get on Harry"?

"Don't Harry me sergeant," I yelled at him "And stand to attention when you address an officer. Is that understood?"

"Why you balmy, snipe nosed, stuck-up, impudent young bastard" he rattled off with a laugh, then added, "Glad you were pleased with the results, sir."

"Well, seriously, you know how it is Ted, good feelings while it all goes on, but at the end of the day it depends if you fill the mould, if you see what I mean."

"Yes" said Ted, "I know exactly what you mean, but you made the attempt Harry and it might come off, you have bloody well earned it, but I know what you mean. Good luck with it mate."

A month had passed before I received the news I was now longing for, 'Proceed to England in two day's time.' My battalion was to go up to the front line tonight, as relief to the troops in place there. Surely they would not expect me to go? I had so often learned of people, homeward bound within one or two days, who were sent out on some minor patrol or other, never to return.

I was afraid of that possibility. However, they did expect me to go and I had no choice. Disappointed beyond belief, I marched away with the battalion, to take over the relief. No looking out over the parapet for me tonight. No more volunteering for patrols. It was lay-low night for me.

The front line at eleven pm, two young officers came over to me, one of them said:

"We are taking a patrol out sergeant and want you to come with us."

"If you would excuse me this time sir," I answered, "I request you leave me off it on this occasion, I go to England in two day's time."

"I'm awfully sorry," he replied, "But we are so short of NCOs, we have no alternative, you will have to be with us!"

When the time arrived, the first officer led the way over-the-top, standing bolt upright, a revolver in one hand and a compass in the other, with the second officer accompanying him. I followed, well to the rear. There was a sudden surprise burst of fire from a German outpost. As I dived flat to the ground, a mad scamper took place around me. The firing ceased, the patrol had totally vanished and I was alone.

After crawling backwards for at least fifty yards, I was challenged by a familiar voice coming from the depths of a shell hole. It was our leader.

"Who are you?" He asked

"The sergeant you almost prevented going to England!" I replied.

"Look here sergeant, if you know the best way back to our trench lead on."

"How about your patrol sir?" I felt obliged to ask. "We can hardly go back without them, can we?"

"Damn the patrol, I expect they're already back in the trench anyhow," he snapped back at me. "If you know the way, lead on, I've lost my damned compass!"

On this occasion my eagerness to get back unscathed, needed no further persuasion and we were back in our own lines virtually within two minutes. The shell hole he had been hiding in when I found him was no more than twenty yards from his own dugout.

175

Re-entering our own trench, we discovered that every man, including the other officer, had already returned. It must have been about three hours later, when a young private came up to me and said

"Sergeant, in that patrol we were out on, I dropped my rifle when they fired at us, and in the panic came back without it, what should I do?"

I know what I should have done. From information like that, he should have gone on report, but I felt so sorry for him. It seemed a long time ago, but I was once as daft as that.

"Do you know what this means?" I asked, "Because if you don't, I will tell you. It will be regarded as cowardice in the face of the enemy, it will mean military disgrace and a court martial." The tears welled in his eyes as he asked

"Is there anything I can do?" Like an idiot, I replied, "Yes, you can follow me!" Had I refused to help him, I would have had it on my conscience that I might have prevented it happening, but didn't.

He supposed we were going to see the officer but as we got closer to the parapet, I said to him quietly, "We are going back out there to fetch your rifle, follow me closely, do as I do and keep silent." I knew the terrain backwards, every stick, stone and roll of wire. I knew the precise spot that we had occupied when the Germans opened fire and that was where we went. Crawling out and crawling back, my way!

We went out, found the rifle and got back without a single shot being fired and were not seen by either side. He was extremely grateful and that was thanks enough for me. I was pleased to have saved him from the disgrace.

It was confirmed to me a short time later that a court martial would indeed have been faced. The captain sent for me to go to his dugout.

"Sergeant Morgan" he began, "I am afraid your journey to England will have to be delayed for some considerable time."

"Has it been cancelled sir?"

"No, it hasn't been cancelled. Not yet at least. But it may be! It seems that two men belonging to last night's patrol have lost their rifles. As you are aware it means a courts martial for them and you will have to stay here to give evidence, as you were the senior NCO on the patrol, I am told."

Damnation, I thought to myself, I can't let this happen. I have to make that trip. 'Think Harry think.' At least they only had two culprits and not three.

"Sir, may I ask what the patrol officers report stated?"

"You know better than that, sergeant; you may not ask!"

"Very well sir, the England trip can wait, if I am needed here. Presumably, I will be expected to tell the exact truth, the way it all happened?"

"Of course you will tell the truth. What is your meaning?"

"I mean just this sir," I said firmly, with a cold intonation. "That the officers were the first to run, the proof was evident. As I crawled backwards towards our lines, I found the first officer in a shell hole behind me. He asked me to guide him back. In response to my enquiry concerning the position of his patrol, his exact reply was: 'Damn the patrol, I suppose they are all back at the trench anyhow.' He then instructed me to guide him home, as his compass had been lost.

The shell hole he was in was a mere twenty yards, or two minutes, from our trench. The second officer meanwhile was found to be already in the trench when we arrived, together with all the men. He had in fact been there for some considerable time sir. The truth is, that the men simply followed the second officer in, because the first officer, was lost in a shell hole twenty yards from home base!"

He was stunned. He looked at me hard as I gave the screw a final twist. "That will have to be my truthful observation, sir"

"Sergeant; just keep your mouth shut, will you? I will see you tomorrow morning, goodnight."

The next morning, he met me in the trench. "Oh, Sergeant Morgan, I've been looking everywhere for you, I really don't see any reason, thinking about it, why you should stay here until tonight. Of course your trip to England is important. With all the pressures of other events, I had overlooked the reason for it. You can pack up at once and report to battalion HQ and I wish you the best of luck;"

I packed, visited all my pals to say goodbye, and set off down the communication trench and away to Batt.HQ to collect my travel papers.

Pack up your troubles in your old kit bag and smile, smile, smile,
While you've a Lucifer to light your fag
Smile boys that's the style,
What's the use of worrying, it never was worth while, so
Pack up your troubles in your old kit bag and smile, smile, smile.

Thirty Five

England and the War Office

January 1918

With my papers all to hand, I was happy to start my journey through France. I never learned the fate of the two unfortunate lads who lost their rifles in the panic of that patrol fiasco. They were not the only ones to panic and as the first officer's compass was government issue, he should have been punished for losing that.

It is quite probable that if the officers had carried rifles, there would have been even more weapon losses. Although, perhaps if that had been the case, they would have sent me out to recover them!

At the coast, I boarded a troopship bound for Dear Old Blighty. A branch of the War Office in Parliament Street, London, had to be my first call. I reported there with my papers and was given three weeks leave and more papers.

During this happy period at home, I learned from my parents, with great relief, that all of my brothers had so far survived, except for wounds. Of course information was not instantaneous, and letters from the front were few. The important point was that no official notification had been received, and for the family to have gone this far, with six of us out there, was indeed rare.

With this good news in my heart, I called in to see Eli and Sarah Hill, Fred's mum and dad, to find out where he was, how he was, and when we were likely to meet up for a big celebration and a bike ride.

It became the saddest moment in my life. They were heartbroken: Freddy had been killed in action, on Saturday 15 July 1916, during a battle on the Somme. It was that same First Battle of the Somme, but another part, in which I had received my second wound on Friday 14 July 1916. That was the day before his death, when we made our daylight attack.

I recalled only too readily, that whilst lying out in No-Man's-Land near the German wire, I had thought of Fred. Where was he? Was he in France waiting to go into battle like me? Was he in a trench on another front, or even another part of the same front? All these things had played on my mind.

He was at that time then, still alive, with just a few hours yet to live! We *were* in the same area, for the same battle, without knowing it. Our different divisions were in action at different parts of the same front.

With the 2nd Batt; R.War.R (the 22nd Brigade of the 7th Division) he would have been in action during the Battle for Bazentin Ridge (14-17 July) that could have been where he died.

I was at Contalmaison then, so we were not too far apart, perhaps distanced by just a short bike ride. Sitting quietly, I saw again the sad image of his expression on that day we were split up, 11 October 1914. The parade on the square at Budbrooke. The handshake as we said goodbye. "So long Fred, don't worry, I'll see you over there" I had said excitedly, as the Regimental Band played me away with "The Warwickshire Lads and Lassies."

That sad, sad face. Those misty eyes remaining in spite of my thoughtlessly reassuring wink, as I marched past him. He never shared my delight or pleasure at that time, and I never fully appreciated his sadness. We can never again repeat our brotherly friendship. I was ashamed of my past action, but not of my present tears. God Bless you 1554, my greatest pal. Sorry mate: I really thought we would both live forever!

If I should die, think only this of me
That there's some corner of a foreign field that is forever England
There shall be, in that rich earth, a richer dust concealed
A dust whom England bore, shaped, made aware
Gave once her flowers to love, her Ways to roam
A body of England's, breathing English air
Washed by the rivers, blessed by Sons of home.

Rupert Brooke (1887 - 1915)

Hill 60 - Passchendaele, where Hal was taken prisoner by the Germans. Today it still stands, as the battle left it, with Pill Boxes and Craters bearing witness to the bloody conflict it provoked.

The rebuilt Cloth halls and Cathedral of YPRES. Reconstructed to the original plans, with just a few adjustments to make good some known problems with the earlier original buildings. The town decided to rebuild rather than leave the ruins as a monument, to show that it's people had not been conquered, nor had their spirit been crushed.

The imposing Memorial at Thiepval, Somme, France, on which 1554 Freddy is listed. there are a vast number of small cemeteries along the route of the original front Line at intervals of just a few hundred yards, it being expedient to bury excessive numbers near the area in which they fell. This particularly huge and impressive monument on the D73 off the main Bapaume to Albert Road (D929), is something 'Our Harry' never knew about, until much later in his life.

Thirty Six

Officer Training Programme

February 1918

A most enjoyable leave and so good to see Liz again, our meetings were now more precious. The shattering news of Fred has brought home the vulnerability of my wartime situation. My overall attitude had now been readjusted somewhat. Liz promised a happy future, and what happened to Fred, was a frightening example of how delicately balanced my life really was.

Orders were received to proceed to Chiseldon, for an attachment to the London Scottish, for part one of my Officer Training Programme. There were about forty NCOs on the course, and we were all placed in the same squad to be drilled by the RSM. He was without a doubt the smartest man I had ever seen on any parade ground.

Immaculate in dress, faultless with command and a credit to the British army. In a short time, we were moving around that parade ground like clockwork. It was a good feeling. At last the Army was going to repay me for some of the gross work I had carried out, they were finally going to elevate my status, and reward my considerable efforts to make progress.

The subjects of the training course were many and varied, musketry, map reading, use of compass, drill principles, section and battalion, as well as the usual educational exams. Some of these sessions included a period whereby we had to drill the men ourselves, which was great fun. I was doing my turn with a squad on the parade ground, at about 11.30 a.m. on the day that Liz had arranged to come down to spend my free afternoon with me.

I liked putting the squad through their paces with foot drill. It gave me the opportunity of yelling at someone and letting off steam. Having taken the column diagonally across the parade ground, I suddenly noticed the trim figure of Liz, standing at the side of the square. What an opportunity! Much too good a chance to miss.

Giving the men a command sequence to bring the column in a straight line along the top edge, followed by a "**RIGHT—WHEEL**," positioned them to the side of the square where Liz was standing.

As they approached, close to her, from her right, I could see the embarrassed look on her face, as she took a small step backwards. This however was nothing compared to the look on her dear face when they drew level, at about two feet distance, and I gave the order "**EYES LEFT.**"

As she explained later, the comments and chat from the men as they marched by, ranged from single low whistles to "How about a date darling." I counted on this of course and before dismissing the squad I told them how badly they had let me down in front of my Missus, who had just taken all their whistles and suggestions. This expectedly resulted in hoots of laughter: Liz forgave me of course!

We shared a fine afternoon together before getting back to the rail station for her train. As far as the training was concerned, it all went well. We were delighted when we all passed out with flying colours. I already had the required qualifications for machine gun and bombing, not to mention a considerable amount of practical experience under fire. My hopes were therefore high and expectations were even higher.

Arrangements were being made, they said, for us to join an intake at a Cadet School, we were told to wait a while. We waited for a few weeks and carried on with whatever general duties they found for us, until eventually a senior officer collected us together in one of the training rooms.

It seems however, that the army were not reliable in this respect either. He regretted to advise us, that too many men from France had been accepted for commission training and our whole contingent of hopefuls would now be re-posted to reserve battalions.

In other words, forget it lads, we made another cock-up. All my great hopes of rising from the ranks were now dashed. I was ordered to report, with four others of my regiment, to Gosforth Park, near Newcastle-On-Tyne.

No point getting worked up about it, this certainly wasn't the only mistake of administration made during the war, and it most certainly was not the most tragic, except perhaps for me!

My disappointment was extreme. There had been little enough visible appreciation shown for my efforts at the front, and because I liked the army, I would have liked to find a future in it. If a small commission had been offered, I really felt that I could have been a useful asset. Did experience not carry any value after all? I seriously believed that a school tie would have qualified!

Settling down to training troops for serving in France was my task at this point, yet after only two weeks of this, the army provided yet another shock to my system. The orderly sergeant came over to my tent to tell me

"Sergeant, you are to prepare for draft leave!" So! It seems that if all else fails, they can shove me back out to France, I am still expendable, I could not bloody believe it! After all I had gone through. This, I intended to fight. I went direct to the captain:

"Excuse me sir," I began, "I have just been warned for draft leave."

"What about it?"

"I have been in France since October 1914 and I have only been back here in England for a few weeks. You have any amount of NCO's in this camp who have never served outside the shores of this country, surely the army can be a little more fair than that, what the hell do they think I am?"

"I take your point sergeant, leave it with me and carry on as usual."

'Our Harry' in Ceremonial Dress uniform at Budbrooke Barracks.
Taken by H.L. Young Studio, 29 Coten End, Warwick.

tune of :-John Brown's Body

One Staff Officer jumped right over another Staff Officers back, and
Another Staff Officer jumped right over that other Staff Officers back
A third Staff Officer jumped right over two other Staff Officers backs
And a fourth Staff Officer jumped right over the other Staff Officers backs.
They were only playing leap-frog, They were only playing leap-frog,
They were only playing leap-frog,
when one Staff Officer jumped right over another Staff Officers back.

Thirty Seven

Try Again Sergeant

July 1918

Having been successfully struck off that draft list I stayed where I was, training troops for the front. Some time in July, I heard that a few sergeants were wanted, to join the King's African Rifles, a regiment of coloured troops who were fighting in East Africa. I put my name down for this and was accepted, sent for a medical, passed fit by the MO and sent to Aldershot in Surrey, for training.

The training was quite difficult, particularly the study of "Swahili." A second language was something I had never attempted before, but I felt I was making headway. Somewhere there must be an opening for me, after all, the majority of people with my experience and training, were now injured or dead! Who knows, maybe this will lead to an opportunity of some sort.

Receiving a 'First Class' pass gave me great delight and I returned to Newcastle to await further orders from the War Office. Upon receipt of official instruction, we would be sent to London, to be kitted-out for Africa. In the meantime I was being sent all over England on escort duty.

Escort duties involved taking or collecting prisoners from, or to, their respective battalions when their terms of imprisonment started or ended. Collecting deserters, who had been rounded up by the Military Police, and escorting them back to their regiments, was also part of my task. It made a change and was far better than the trenches.

Whilst waiting for the results of my application, I went home on leave for a longer period, to put into action something that Liz and I had been contemplating for some time. I proposed marriage. Whilst I was at such great risk in Belgium and France, I felt it would be wrong to consider marriage, but now that I appeared to have finished with that part of the war, it seemed safe to go ahead.

It was anticipated some time ago and Liz and I had talked about it on my visits home. Her brother Hal had been taken prisoner at Hill 60 after a fierce battle there, and had been moved to a prison camp in Germany. I wrote to him on 16 April 1918 through International Red Cross, to ask if he would be our Best Man.

I have no idea when it reached him, but I received a reply stamped 5 July 1918. It was on an official German card, which bore a UK received postmark of 10 August 1918, and delivered to my parent's house in Peel Street. In it, he said he would be delighted to accept, but had no idea at all when he might be released. It was not to be. With his elder brother Bill standing in for him, I was able to arrange further leave for September. On Saturday 14 of that month 1918, just sixty-nine days before my 23rd birthday, and when Liz was only twenty-three days from her 22nd birthday, we were married at Christ Church, Summerfield, Birmingham.

The Wedding group after the ceremony, in the tiny backyard of 150, Peel Street.
Back row - L to R - Nell Rogers - Louise Rogers - Father of Harry - Lizzie Morgan - Bill Rogers - James Rogers (father)
Centre - Mother of Harry - Our Harry - Liz - Mother of Liz - Alice Beck (wife of Hal Rogers)
Front - Polly Morgan - Amelia morgan - Gladys ? - Nell (wife of Frank Morgan) and daughter Nellie Morgan

189

Just two months after this happy event, another most wonderful thing happened- **The War Ended!**

With it of course ended my opportunity to go with The King's African Rifles, as the situation had now changed and the sergeants were not required. But the war being at an end was a much greater event, and we were all feverishly excited. We had won, our fighting days were over and we could now think about all the exciting things we would start to do. The jobs we would be able to get. The money we could earn!

What of the war? At the eleventh hour, of the eleventh day, of the eleventh month, 1918. It just stopped! No one really won anything. No one seemed to have lost anything. It proved or solved little. It did succeed however, in killing 8,538,315 men and wounding 21,219,452.

Tune of:- "They'll never believe me"

And when they ask us what did you do in the war ?
Oh we'll never tell them, No we'll never tell them,
We sat around in some cafe
And fought wild women night and day
'twas the cushiest job we ever knew,
And when they ask us, and they're certainly going to ask us
The reason why we didn't win the Croix de Guerre
Oh we'll never tell them, no we'll never tell them
There was a Front, but damned if we knew where.

Thirty Eight

AFTER THE WAR IS OVER.

Exciting though it was, that my family had six sons engaged in front line battle areas, with cavalry, infantry and artillery regiments. It was almost unbelievable that all six of us finally returned in reasonable health, after just a few wounds, and troublesome though these were for some time later, we were all alive. I was given my three campaign medals, which I was pleased to receive, they were hereafter always to be known by the troops as 'Pip, Squeak and Wilfred,' named after a cartoon series running in a newspaper at that time. Three little dogs, I think they were. The medals were the 1914 Mons Star, the British War Medal (1914 -1918) and the Victory Medal (1914-1919). Pity about the possible DCM.[3]

In 1930 I visited Highbury hospital for an X-ray.

"Do you know," they said, "You have a piece of metal in your leg"

"Get away" I replied, "Would you believe that?"

They operated and after fourteen years, it was removed. I had a spell in hospital and time off from work, with the resultant loss of pay, for a total of 7 weeks. Unfortunately, I had no contact with the bloody old fool of a medic who insisted that it was not there. I could have posted it to him.

Later in life I was able to visit the huge Thiepval Memorial, Somme.

Sadly my dear old pal Fred had no grave. His body was never found, but his name is carved with pride on the massive Royal Warwickshire Regt. Pier (9A, 9B & 10B) stating simply - '1554, Private Frederick Hill, aged 20 - died 15th July 1916.' It is a large and imposing construction, designed by Sir Edward Lutyens. Fred is in good company there, but none of them deserved to die.

---

[3] see Appendix three

Hal Rogers was released from Germany fit and healthy, wounds healed, bringing with him three beautiful white polo neck sweaters. One for me, one for 'Big' Jim and one for himself.

He exchanged Red Cross parcel soap, for both the wool, and the ability of a German guard, who taught him to knit. The sweaters were superb and I still have mine today, well worn, but in excellent condition. It has elaborate rope stitch, ladder stitch, cable stitch, and others. Using 15 needles, all branching out in different directions to form arms, body, neck etc. in one piece. No sewing and no seams.

Someone I knew well, Gil Merrick, goalkeeper for Birmingham City, wanted me to sell it to him. I couldn't do that however, it was too precious.

Hal married his girl friend Alice and after joining the Birmingham Branch of the Seaforth Highlanders Association, became one of their most useful organisers. He became, in addition to this, a tireless committee member or secretary, to an astonishing number of clubs and societies.

'Big' Jim Rogers also arrived home safe and well. He settled into what for him was normal. Entertaining, writing and producing shows at the drop of anybody's hat. He later toured the country with a concert party where his talents were much in demand.

In fact every member of both families found a lifelong partner in marriage, but whereas we Morgans' were more introvert and reserved, the Rogers' outlook was far different.

I really think that my connection with the Rogers family helped me to overcome the difficulties that faced us after the war, insurmountable though the problems sometimes appeared to be. Every free weekend was party time. They *were* the party, the entertainment, the light-hearted life and soul. It was impossible to be dull and dreary around them.

A large family also, Bill, Jim, Hal, Jack and George, with the girls, Liz, Louise and Nell. The entertainment bug however, hit just Bill, Jim, Hal and Liz, who went together around the local pubs as teenagers. After asking consent of the Manager, with one foot in the door, they would put on their show for the customers, and go round with a hat. They all had fine singing voices. In fact the eldest of the family, Bill, was heard by a top comedian of the day, named Sandy Powell, who was so impressed, that he suggested Bill should be professionally trained for opera. "Tour the halls with me," he said, "as part of my act, just to sing and give a musical lift, and I will pay for the tuition." Mr Powell even went to see James Rogers, Bill's dad. The answer was a definite, "NO! He has to stay and help look after the family, like the rest of them."

For them, entertainment started as a necessity in order to increase family income beyond the low earning power of their father. A large family needs income. They were natural, professional, talented, loving and supportive. It was difficult to know sometimes where life started and humour began. My real introduction to their humour was, strangely, at 'Big' Jim's wedding.

He escorted his young wife Bess to the altar at St. Patrick's church, Winson Green, and then on to the small reception at their house. After the meal and halfway through the festivities, the bride was looking for Jim, then everyone was looking for Jim. He had not been seen at all for some time, and neither had the Best Man. Bess was quite worried until someone came up to her and said, "Please don't be worried Bess, I wouldn't tell you this if you were less concerned, but he's just had to slip away for a while."

This was no consolation to Bess, who was now distraught. "Why? Why?" she begged, "Why did he do it?" Jim's friend could see that he had no alternative other than to admit, "The Villa are playing at home today."

There was immediately a total silence, Bess standing with gaping mouth, the rest of us frozen in wonderment, and disbelief. It was only when Hal said "He's sure to be back for your honeymoon, Bess," that the penny dropped. The laughter raised the roof, but the new bride found it difficult to raise a smile.

In spite of this somewhat precarious start, it must be said that they proved to be an ideal combination. They shared a happy life together, giving birth to a strong healthy male child, destined to carry with him for a lifetime, the equally uninspired family name of 'Little' Jim.

My brass box gift, from the Princess Mary also made it home intact. It now contains locks of little golden curls taken from the shortened hair of my daughter Betty who was born in 1926. The curls were cut when she was four years old. The photograph of the Princess got lost, the Christmas card was badly damaged, the pipe broken and the tobacco and cigarettes have long since been smoked.

We had a little boy in 1929 named Arthur. Another one born never to use the names given at birth. Liz did not like the name Arthur, but as we were at the time living with my father, whose name it was, she agreed that it would be a nice gesture to him, but admitted that she would never use it. He therefore became an Arthur Edward, who for many years was known only as Sonny.

I could at first only get part time employment, and Jim arranged for me to do shift work, on night duty at the Dudley Road Hospital where he worked. It went quite well, though I knew little of nursing, or of being an orderly, but

Princess mary's gift to the soldiers at the Front, with curls from the head of daughter Betty.

it was far better than selling matches on the street. One night however, the young girl nurse I was working with, was tending a young male patient about 25 yrs of age, when he hit her full in the face. She fell to the ground and I responded, as trained to do instinctively, by hitting the patient who also fell to the ground. The nurse got to her feet, but the patient didn't. Doctor and Sister came in at a run and placed the man on a bed, tended him first, then attended the nurse. I had the sack!

Then I went to Bulpitt and Sons, a Birmingham Company with the well-known 'Swan Brand' trademark, where I became a metal spinner. I made saucepans and kettles from aluminium blanks. It employed me, and kept the family for a number of years, but I hated the job. Aluminium is such a filthy metal to work with.

A spare time job as barman at the Queens Head in Aberdeen Street, kept me sane, was enjoyable, and helped out with some extra income. It was managed by the Billingsley family, who were long standing family friends. How strange that all those years ago, when I was a member of their Cycling Club with my father, that I would have gone to hell and back, before finishing up as a part time Barman there!

Eventually, I left Bulpitts' and the filthy aluminium, to take on the Management of a Public House with Mitchell's and Butlers Brewery, Cape Hill. We were allocated the Woodbine Stores, in Washington Street,

Birmingham. My first Pub in 1939 which was, without a doubt the strangest little Pub with the most endearing, charming and surprisingly unusual customers you ever could meet: And guess what! Someone started another bloody **WAR.** You see, they never do learn, do they! This one I would have to fight as a civilian.

Cards sent to Liz, of silk, embroidered or hand coloured photographs. Sentiments move from 'Thinking of you' to 'God bless you' and 'Fondest Love' to 'My sweetheart'. and finally 'My dear Wife' Liz kept them all!

Appendix

1.   Gift from HRH The Princess Mary.

Her Royal Highness The Princess Victoria Alexandra Alice Mary was the third child and only daughter, of King George V and Queen Mary. Born on 25 April 1897 she was 17 when war broke out.

Wanting to pay, out of her private allowance, for a personal gift to be sent to all soldiers and sailors, her advisers indicated many reasons why this would not be possible. They suggested that she lent her name to a National fund for the purpose.

A committee was formed and the decision made, to produce a brass box to hold various items for the smoker. Messrs Adshead and Ramsay designed it, with the hinged lid bearing a portrait effigy of the Princess surrounded by a laurel, either side of which was the letter M stylised as her monogram. At the top was a representation of a bayonet and scabbard, with a central legend 'Imperium Britannicum.'

The bottom displayed the legend, 'Christmas 1914' with side images of two bows of dreadnought battleships. Each corner, and both sides bore the names of the allies:- France, Belgium, Japan, Russia, Serbia and Montenegro, with their flags.

First to receive them, were those under Class A, The Navy, and Troops at the front in France. The distribution on Christmas Day, had been 426,724 gifts.' The revised estimate for those finally eligible was in excess of two million.

2.   First Battle of the Somme 01 July, 1916

A creeping barrage was planned, with the guns being aimed first at the enemy wire to blast it away, then lifting to the front line itself, in order to crush the trenches and annihilate the enemy, then to be gradually lifted again, in order to hit the support trenches further back, and prevent support troops moving forward. This way, the barrage would be continuously moving back, to unroll a 'carpet' of shells.

It was calculated that if the British force moved too fast, they would outpace their own artillery and run into British fire. They were therefore instructed to walk at a measured pace, and follow the barrage, moving forward at a safe distance.

The massive build-up to the battle and the overlong bombardment had destroyed any element of surprise. Furthermore, In spite of the concentrated shelling of the enemy lines, the shells directed at the wire were light, and of an 'impact' explosion classification. Many of these simply bounced on the wire, not to explode, and in places severely flattened it, providing a more solid defence for the enemy than it previously was.

Massive bombardment with the heavier guns did not smash the enemy trenches, which were 20ft to 30ft deep, reinforced with concrete. Well-armed, German forces were still established in the forward trench, and the creeping barrage lifted too early, going over their heads.

Pip, Sqeak and Wilfred showing a silver rose on the Mons Star ribbon.

Communications of the day were such, that the artillery could not be advised of the problem. By adhering to the original plan, the guns lifted at a rate not possible for the advancing troops to match. Hampered by the wire, and carrying their 66lb packs, their pace slowed down, leaving their straight lined ranks, an easy target for the German machine guns, now reassembled within the untouched front line trenches.

3.   PIP, SQUEAK and WILFRED

The Daily Mirror on 12 May 1919 ran a cartoon strip written by B.J.Lamb and drawn by A.B.Payne. Payne used to call his batman 'Pip-squeak' and thought the split name could make up two of the characters. Pip became a dog, and Squeak a penguin. Somehow, at a later stage they gave birth to a rabbit named Wilfred.

There was then another penguin named Auntie with additional characters along the way. The popularity of the series was so strong that the three campaign medals were affectionately given the names, by Servicemen.

1914 Star	**Bronze with a central scroll marked Aug. - Nov. 1914** Issued to members of the BEF serving in France and Belgium between 5 August 1914 and 22 November 1914. Sometimes called the Mons Star.
Additions	A bar or clasp, was approved by King George V, on 19 Oct. 1919, for all holders of the medal serving 'under fire.' Sewn on the ribbon, it was bronze, bearing the dates 5th Aug - 22nd Nov 1914. If the ribbon on its own was worn, a small silver rose sewn to the ribbon indicated possession of the clasp.
1914/15 Star	**Bronze with a different scroll marked - 1914 - 15** Issued to others serving in theatres of war between 5 Aug. 1914 and 31 Dec. 1915. (not BEF).
British War Medal	**Solid Silver Dated 1914 and 1918** St. George equestrian trampling the 'Central Powers' Shield. Issued to all who served within the three armed services.

Victory Medal   **Bronze Dated 1914 - 1918**
Winged victory holding a palm branch on the front, and on the reverse, the words 'The Great War for Civilisation.' Awarded to holders of 1914 Star, 1914 - 1915 Star, and most holders of the British War Medal. It could not be awarded on its own.